19: Spain in Transition:
Prospects and Policies

To my daughter Jessica

THE WASHINGTON PAPERS
Volume II

19: Spain in Transition:
Prospects and Policies

ARNOLD HOTTINGER

THE CENTER FOR STRATEGIC AND INTERNATIONAL STUDIES
Georgetown University, Washington, D.C.

SAGE PUBLICATIONS
Beverly Hills / London

RS
G46.082 HOTT
145617

For information address:

SAGE PUBLICATIONS, INC.
275 South Beverly Drive
Beverly Hills, California 90212

SAGE PUBLICATIONS LTD
St George's House / 44 Hatton Garden
London EC1N 8ER

International Standard Book Number 0-8039-0205-0

Library of Congress Catalog Card No. 74-21523

FIRST PRINTING

*When citing a Washington Paper, please use the proper form. Remember to cite
the series title and include the paper number. One of the two following formats
can be adapted (depending on the style manual used):*

(1) HASSNER, P. (1973) "Europe in the Age of Negotiation." The Washington
Papers, I, 8. Beverly Hills and London: Sage Pubns.

OR

(2) Hassner, Pierre. 1973. *Europe in the Age of Negotiation.* The Washington
Papers, vol. 1, no. 8. Beverly Hills and London: Sage Publications.

CONTENTS

INTRODUCTORY NOTE

This is the second part of a study on contemporary Spain, dealing with the main political forces active in that country today. Part I, published as Washington Paper Number 18, covers the legacy of the Civil War and the process of Spain's adaptation to the postwar world, to social and economic developments, to changes inside the Church, and to events on the domestic scene up to the assassination of Prime Minister Carrero Blanco in December 1973.

PREFACE TO PART II OF "SPAIN IN TRANSITION"

From the legal to the real country. Almost every country suffers from a gap between the legal state and the real nation. The divergence results basically from the fact that the system of legal rules and ordinances trails by definition behind the mobile pattern of social evolution. But in few countries of the Western world are the disparities greater than in Spain, due to the circumstance that in Spain the legal and political systems were decreed in the wake of the Civil War by those victorious in that conflict. The system has evolved somewhat since 1939, but within narrow limits imposed by the workings of internal power. Essentially the legal and political systems continue to serve as the means of guaranteeing and perpetuating the power of the victors in the Civil War.

The legal country thus has remained anchored within the framework of the corporative state of the postwar period. The partisans of the regime tend to envisage this framework as the "eternal Spain" embodying the "essential values of Spain." Yet the real country has evolved significantly in the last 35 years. Biologically most present-day Spaniards belong to a generation which did not participate in the Civil War. Economically the country advanced decisively in the decade after 1959. In the realm of ideas, the younger generation of Spaniards is on the whole much closer to the thinking of contemporary Europeans than to the ideas of their fathers. Consequently Spain today offers the picture of a society constantly pressing against limits of the political and legal framework imposed in a different past and not apparently in harmony with present-day Spanish society.

This is recognized, in theory, by the ruling circles themselves; they speak of the need for political and social evolution, and they have made many promises in this spirit. But they are caught in a dilemma: should they put their promises into practice, they risk losing their power. Consequently they tend toward partial liberalization which frequently, in implementation, bears only the trappings of liberalization.

Beneath the screen of apparent and belated liberalization and modernization, the real country continues to evolve and to change. The contrast, ever sharpening, between the realities of life and the fictions of legality helps spawn many kinds of political groupings that function illegally or at the edges of legality. The contrast also prompts the influx of political ideas into basically nonpolitical groups, such as religious societies, cultural clubs, associations of friends, groupings of learned people, professional associations, students and pupils clubs, folklore groupings, artistic groups, and even bookshops and art galleries.

All these political and crypto-political groups functioning in the twilight of legality or completely underground are reflections of the real country asserting itself against the legal state. This is why they are significant and must be regarded as signposts to the future. If they can muster the force to affirm themselves in face of legal injunctions and frequent police persecution, they must stand for things which significant segments of Spain desire or judge necessary.

This does not mean that all the aims embraced by the political and crypto-political groups can be realized. Especially in light of the diversity of these aims, at best there will have to be compromises. In the worst case one or the other groups will manage to impose its will upon the whole community with authoritarian means. In practical terms, this would require the help of the army, since the army is very much the ultimate source of power in Spain.

Against this background, the groups and factions to the right of the Spanish spectrum stand the best chance at present to prevail in a post-Franco Spain. The groups in the center and to the left face the task of extending their influence with the hope of eventual triumph—assuming that they will be able to expand their influence without provoking the army and, to a lesser degree, the police. Some of the left wing groups have recognized this fact of political life in Spain, notably the Communist Party. Others remain obstinate in refusing to admit them. They continue to dream of a people's revolution that would split the army horizontally and enlist the rank-and-file soldiers. The center groups hope fervently for a gradual evolution toward democracy which would safeguard law and order and thus avoid provoking the armed forces.

The actual victor of Spanish evolution will have to await the crucible of future events. For the present, any analyst can only try to enumerate and evaluate the different groups and nuclei of political tendencies, to the extent that these appear through the fog of illegality and official repression.

4

I. THE CURRENT POLITICAL GROUPINGS

Falangists

Among the different political groups which exist in Spain at present and which will inevitably have some influence on the developments of the future, the Falange must take pride of place, if for no other reason than because it represents the only legally recognized political group. Having made this statement, one has to modify it. The Falange does not have any legal existence in Spain since it has been absorbed into the Movement, *el Movimiento Nacional.* But on the other hand, the Falange has not been proscribed either. Its representatives say that it cannot be, because it has an historical legitimacy, by which they mean its role in the Civil War and before that.

In political practice, the Spaniards distinguish between at least two Falanges. There is what can be called the Old Guard—the blue shirts, the "old shirts", the historical Falange, Franco's guard, the ideological Falange, the hard-liners, the ultras, those who hanker for the past, etc. This means either old people who live in and with their memories of the Civil War, or a younger fringe that has been captivated by the myths and ideology of that era. On the other hand, there is what can be called the Falange of the establishment, the bureaucratic Falange or *Movimiento*—the opportunists, the *movimiento-gobierno* (as opposed to *movimiento-ideología*), the wielders of power who happen to be of Falangist origin, to have a Falangist clientèle, or to have used, more or less intentionally, the Falangist ideology and organizations to achieve positions of influence and power.

The "hankerers" are easy to describe. They were active as youths in the ranks of the Falange and they continue to believe in the mythology they were taught at the time of the Civil War or in the first ten years following it. Many of them now find themselves outside active politics. They are frequently small bureaucrats. They may, for instance, be provincial delegates of the Madrid ministries, particularly the Ministry of the Interior (which nominates a large hierarchy of provincial dignitaries, from the provincial governors downward); or they may be in the police or the professional officers' corps. You can find them, too, among the priests, as a result of the persecution of clerics during the Civil War, and in the professions.

Most nostalgic Falangists naturally tend to be older people who lived through the Civil War. But just as there have been fringes of neo-fascists among the young in other European countries, there are some youth groups in Spain, perhaps mostly in the universities, who have been influenced by the myths of the past. While they cannot be said to have a coherent ideology, they want to imitate the deeds of their elders, carrying pistols, fighting street battles and attempting to punish "Jews, freemasons and reds." With regard to such fringe groups, Spain is not really different from other European countries, say Italy or even Belgium, except that in Spain they arrogate to themselves the historical rights claimed by the older generation they are imitating.

This older generation helped to win the Civil War, and its members consider the state rightfully theirs, even though they have been unjustly denied the power they regard as their due. Their "rights" are recognized by the state and state agencies, such as the police, at least in the sense that they are permitted to do certain things which are prohibited to the ordinary citizen. They may, for example, organize protest demonstrations against political developments of which they disapprove strongly; they may hold political reunions; and they may form small groups of vigilantes—for instance at the universities—which often resort to quite violent action. These vigilantes sometimes get the unofficial but effective help of the police, because they are a useful weapon against red students, priests, leftist Catholic groups and so on, which the police may be reluctant to tackle directly.

The hankerers are able to do these things because the lines separating them from their powerful friends and allies, the Falangist administrators, are ill-defined. The National Council of the Movimiento is one place where the old fighters of the Civil War can exert political influence. National Councillors are automatically members of the Cortes. Forty-one National Councillors are named directly by Franco, twelve more by the prime minister, and Franco has made a practice of naming some "old shirts" into the Council. There are also some notable "blue generals" among the top officers. These are becoming fewer as the years go by and the old fighters of the Civil War reach retirement age. General Iniesta Cano, for example, head of the *Guardia Civil*, was due to retire in May 1974. Generals Pérez Viñeta and García Rebull, who played important roles a few years ago, have both gone on the retired list and have hardly been heard of since: the former ended his military career as military governor of Barcelona; the latter as military governor of Madrid. Every province has a military governor, and the post is usually reserved for a senior officer near the end of his service. If martial law is proclaimed, the military governors take over the civilian government of the province; in normal times, they command the local garrisons.

One of the questions which is very relevant for the future of the country concerns the number of officers in the lower ranks who think and react like their elders, even though they themselves did not participate in the Civil War. But it is virtually impossible to find the answer: one must be satisfied with guesswork. There are likely to be more younger officers of that mentality than, say, students or middle-aged professionals, because of the affinities which seem to link the military mind and fascist mythology, and, perhaps even more important, because the military in Spain constitute a fairly close caste. Officers tend to marry other officers' daughters. The military establishment has been exposed less to the winds of change than, for instance, the economic community. Officers are often graduates of the military academies, where the sons of officers enjoy special entry facilities. All this makes for a narrow caste in which one would expect traditions, such as the Falangist one, to last longer than in the country at large.

The same is true of the police and Guardia Civil, whose officers are seconded from the army. The question is of central importance because the Spanish army is thought to regard one of its two principal tasks as being the maintenance of the established order. That being so, it is very important what exactly the officers consider the core of that order and what they believe to be the limits which the civilian society must not overstep in its social and political evolution.

The role of the "administrative Falange" is best understood in historical perspective. The Falange was, until 1966, the state party. People with political ambitions had to join it and be active in its ranks. One of the important nurseries of power in those years was the S.E.U. (the universities syndicate): a student who became one of the leaders in the organization was pretty certain to go on to a political career once he had finished his studies. He might go into the Ministry of the Interior and become assistant governor, and later governor of a province; or he might enter the state syndicates and become the local leader of one of the *sindicatos* at provincial level, rising in due course to national level in the sindicatos bureaucracy. In the years before the economic reform which began in 1957, all kinds of economic positions were also open to young and aspiring Falangists. Typical of the jobs they might expect to land were management positions in the state industrial enterprise, I.N.I., which has been compared to an enormous and all-embracing octopus—until the Opus Dei technocrats got hold of it and started to clip its tentacles. The fact that, under the Opus reform, the economic positions would no longer go to the Falangists but to professionally qualified people, was at the root of the bitter enmity the Falange felt towards the Catholic organizations.

The Falange was never the sole channel to power in Franco's state. Only a small proportion of ministerial posts went to Falangists (more in the war years, fewer later); the other "political families" of the regime were usually considered as well. These were monarchists, frequently connected with the landowners and the banks; traditionalist (Carlists); conservative Catholics, particularily those who had been active in the ranks of the lay movement of propagandists. To the political families Franco was in the habit of adding a sprinkling of technocrats, such as road engineers, mostly people who had gone through one of the big and prestigious professional schools, or who had made their way up through the competitive university examinations (*oposiciones*) into the various professional and legal elites—professionals such as state economists, university professors, advocates, notaries, financial technologists, and architects.

The Falangists of the administration thus had to rub shoulders with groups of a different outlook and to cooperate with them. They were expected to give their first loyalty to Franco and the administration, not to their Falangist ideology and friends. This was, in practice, a condition for their success in the administration, and they tended over the years to become quite different from their more purist contemporaries who had stayed out of the administration or remained in its lower ranks.

Sindicatos has remained a typically Falangist ministry, because men were and are needed to keep the workers in line. Other ministries with a high proportion of Falangists are the Interior and the three service ministries. In ministries such as Housing and Social Insurance, many meritorious Falangists have found a niche after being removed from the economic ministries when these were taken over by the Opus.

A curious phenomenom that must not be overlooked is the progressive Falangists. Some of the young people with political interests who had been members of Falange institutions, for example the youth movement, *Frente de Juventudes,* later underwent a mildly socialist, somewhat more contemporary or even democratic evolution. They founded political groups such as the "Past Members of the Frente de Juventudes" under Cantarero del Castillo, advocating a democratic and moderately socialist line. Or they formed the more radical *Círculos José Antonio.* which discovered leftist teachings in the writings of José Antonio de la Rivera, the founder of the Falange, and were closed down by the authorities in 1973 because they were considered to have gone too far to the left. After a few months, however, these circles,

whose leading figure is Diego Marques, were permitted to resume
their activities.

The best known groups of the nostalgic section of the Falangists are *Fuerza Nueva*, under the leadership of the lawyer Blas
Piñar, a member of the National Council nominated by Franco.
They have been the chief demonstrators against the Opus, soft
government, and red bishops in recent years. They publish a
vitriolic monthly, and they are said to have connections with the
army and the police forces. The Franco Old Guard, led by Carlos
Pincilla, is in the same category, but is more conformist and less
virulent. Among the hankerers must also be counted the groups
of Civil War veterans such as the temporary officers' brotherhood,
the *Hermandades de alfereces provisionales*. It is these groups of
hankerers for the past that have come out most violently against
the Opus in demonstrations like the very large one staged in
December 1970 after the Burgos trials of the Basque ETA,
carrying slogans such as *Franco si, Opus no!* Arias Navarro's
removal of the Opus ministers when he formed his government in
January 1974 was certainly a source of satisfaction to the nostal-
gists although they were not happy about the promises made by
the new prime minister, on his assumption of office, of future
participation by the Spanish people in politics.

Somewhat on the lunatic fringe—but occasionally winning the
collaboration of the political police—are the various Falangist
groups at the universities. They are: *Frente de Estudiantes Sindi-
calistas* (FES), close to the above-mentioned Past Members of the
Frente de Juventudes; Frente Revolucionario Sindicaliste,
(FRS), further to the left and aiming at a syndicalist state: *Frente
de Estudiantes Nacional Sindicalistas* (FENS), an exclusively
Valencia group, close to AUN (see below); *Frente Universitario
Nacional Sindicalista,* close to the círculos mentioned above;
Fuerza Joven, close to Blas Piñar's Fuerza Nueva; *Sindicato
Español Universitario,* which wants to reconstitute the old SEU;
Acción Universitaria Nacional (AUN), nationalists, critical of the
government; *Guardia de Franco,* similar to AUN: *Acción Demo-
cratica,* anticommunist, close to AUN: *Frente Sindicalista
Revolucionario,* a splinter group from FES. All these groups

together comprise only a small minority of the politically minded minority of students. They serve as attack formations against the many groups of students of the left.

In themselves, the more extreme Falangists are not of great importance today. But it is their presence in the army and the police, to an extent that cannot be gauged, that makes them potentially dangerous and powerful.

The Other Political Families of the Regime

The other groups, or political families, which took part in the nationalist rising under Franco and were therefore admitted into the ruling establishment, have become even more diversified than the Falange. The Monarchists have split into the unconditional followers of Don Juan and those who support the regime and accept, with varying degrees of enthusiasm, the successor nominated by Franco, Don Juan Carlos. This latter attitude is the only legally permitted one. Moreover, since Don Juan himself had made it clear that he is not going to fight for his rights, even though he maintains them, it is difficult for his partisans to declare themselves his followers to the exclusion of his son.

Generally speaking, the Monarchists are members of the nobility, rich in real estate and partly involved, via the banks, in the industrialization of Spain. Their very considerable material interests make it impossible for them not to cooperate with the state in a more or less active fashion. As a result, true monarchism, loyalty to the man regarded as the rightful successor of Spain's last king, Alphonso XIII, is not much more than a nostalgic and romantic attitude, more sentimental than political. In practical politics, the Monarchists are virtually forced to give their support to Franco and his appointed successor, Don Juan Carlos.

This is probably true also of the apparently considerable number of royalist officers. Only if some unforeseen development were to upset Don Juan Carlos' position and return Don Juan to the forefront would it be thinkable that the Monarchist officers could undertake any action in favor of the *Conde de Barcelona*. As long as his son remains the officially proclaimed successor to the throne they will accept and support him even if, in certain cases, with some misgivings and regrets, because in their eyes the rights of his father have been disregarded.

The Church, and with it the Spanish Catholics, has been split in many ways due to discussion raging within Catholic circles. The Catholic groups which collaborated with Franco in the Civil War have gathered around the newspaper *Ya*, which used to speak for the Spanish hierarchy. There were once more active groups, such as the Catholic lay movements, *Acción Nacional de Propagandistas* and the youth and workers groups, which were supposed to do what they could to foster religion in the social and political worlds. But the debates inside the Church had a somewhat negative effect on their development.

In 1967, shortly before the more progressive ideas had begun to prevail in the Bishops' Conference, very restrictive new regulations were formulated for the lay organizations. They took nearly all freedom of action and initiative away from the laymen themselves and gave the hierarchy rigid control. In Catholic circles in Spain these regulations are known as the reactionary regimentation of the lay movements—the adjective sometimes being written with quotation marks, sometimes without. The regulations had a dual effect: they devitalized the official lay institutions of the Church, turning them, in the judgment of many Spanish Catholics, into rather sleepy and passive bodies; and they helped to channel the more energetic and forward-looking Catholic lay forces into the groups of activist and nonconformist *contestatarios* or even left Catholics and Catholic revolutionaries. These groups are definitely outside the regime and consider themselves part of the opposition.

Numerically, the traditional Catholics are undoubtedly by far the biggest group in Spain. But qualitatively, the "progressive" and "compromised" Catholics are increasingly important, because they are the active minority and they attract the sympathies of the youth—insofar as the young people care about the Church at all. The bishops themselves have begun to denounce the routine, sometimes empty, and even pagan aspects of traditional church life in Spain, and to emphasize the need to deepen the religious understanding of the people. Some of them see this mainly as a matter of improving the individual Spaniard's knowledge and understanding of his religion and its teachings. But many of the bishops lay the chief stress on the social aspect of the faith, on the need to make religion a living force in this world and to take a positive stand for what is right and against what is wrong in the social and political fields, as well as in the life of the individual.

All this has led to a tremendous discussion in Spain both within the Church itself and between the government and the different Church groups. The fact that all Spaniards claim to be Catholics and therefore authorized to proclaim, and if need be to fight for, their religious views whatever these may be, brings the ruling establishment into the fray defending—sometimes with considerable violence—the traditional point of view. This is, to put it crudely, that the Catholics in Spain are there to support and laud the state, since the state likes to consider itself the embodiment of Catholicism and the crusading arm of the Church.

Catholicism as a political force has been useful to Franco as in legitimization of his regime, both inside Spain and, after the collapse of the Axis powers in the Second World War, vis-à-vis the outside world. In the critical years after the war he used Catholics, or even people close to Catholic democracy, in the Ministry of Foreign Affairs. When they became too democratic in their views, however, he would replace them with more authoritarian individuals. And when the Church began propagating increasingly liberal views and beliefs in the social field, there was less and less room in the government for Catholics accepting the new doctrines of the Vatican Council, with a tendency toward replacing them with members of Opus Dei.

This great lay organization—*Societas Sacerdotalis Sanctae Crucis,* to give it its official title—was founded in 1928. Its members dedicate themselves to spreading the message of the Church and to the practice of a spiritual life while pursuing their secular avocations. It has always insisted that it is a purely religious association and has nothing to do with politics. Members are said to be entirely free to act in this world as their conscience dictates. This affirmation is borne out by the fact that in politics members of the Opus were to be found not only inside the government but also in the ranks of the opposition—fewer, it is true, but some of them men of significance. The enemies of the Opus wanted to see in this undeniable fact nothing more than a clever trick: it was playing on several chess boards simultaneously, they explained. But in fact there is little doubt that members of the lay order such as Calvo Serer and Antonio Fontán, the two principal figures at the head of the daily "Madrid" (which has been liquidated by the information authorities) had come to "democratic" and "European" ideals by way of a gradual evolution from their earlier, more Falangist points of view. At the end of this road they saw themselves very much as antagonists and political enemies of the Opus people inside the government, principally Lopez Rodó and his school, and the ministers looked on them as enemies in return.

The special strength of the governing group of the Opus was the fact that its representatives were specialists in the economic and managerial fields, something which was difficult to find in the Spain of the fifties and early sixties. But they became much more dispensable once the economic reform had time to throw up a new managerial class with experience in modern business methods and organization. The Opus technocrats could now be replaced by similar experts without any particular affiliation, and this was done in 1973 in the government of Carrero Blanco and—even more completely—in 1974 by his successor, Arias Navarro.

There seems little likelihood that the Opus will have a political comeback in the future. Personalities such as Lopez Rodó, Lopez Bravo, and their like might conceivably return to power. But it seems improbable that we shall ever again see a whole Opus group of ministers such as unquestionably existed in the years between 1957 and 1973. The principal reason for the rise to power of the organization in that period—the virtual monopoly of the Opus in the economic and managerial fields—no longer exists.

Furthermore, the Matesa scandal probably did irreparable harm to the reputation of the Opus as a political force. This was the affair in which the Catalan industrial firm of Matesa used state export credits nominally to sell its weaving machines on the international market, while in fact supplying them to its own subsidiaries in foreign countries. The apparently embezzled credits reached the incredible sum of 10 milliard pesetas (about $166 m. at the time), and the economic ministries, virtually in the hands of the Opus technocrats, had been responsible for handing them out. The scandal broke in 1969 and was quashed by means of an indemnity granted by Franco in 1971. But in retrospect, it seems highly probable that this was responsible for the eventual exit of the Opus politicians in 1973 and 1974. Their Falange enemies had gotten the scandal between their teeth and were not going to drop it until they had used it to destroy most of the Opus credit.

Lastly among the "families of the regime" must be mentioned the Carlists, also called Traditionalists. They represent the followers of the *Carlista* branch of the Spanish monarchy, which split off from the ruling branch at the beginning of the 19th century. During the three Carlist civil wars during that century, Carlism became identified with unshakable, traditional Catholic doctrine and deep regional feelings. Carlism furnished its own militia in the Civil War, the so-called *Requeté*. It has always been strongest in the northern provinces, such as Navarre, the Basque provinces, and Catalonia, but it had some centers in the south as well—Seville and Valencia, for example.

Politically, the Carlists were forcibly united with the Falange by Franco in 1937, but they maintained their own family feeling and their symbol, the Carlist pretender to the throne, who lived in exile in France. By a process of renunciations and transfers of legitimacy, the Carlist succession came to rest, for the majority of the movement, on Don Javier of Borbón-Parma and his son, Don Carlos Hugo. Both were expelled from Spain in 1968 in the course of the preparations for "Operation Juan Carlos".

Even before this time, the younger generation of Carlists had begun to agitate for true syndicates and regional freedom, thus marking the transfer of their support from the regime to the opposition. Carlos Hugo himself had encouraged this line. When his father, Don Javier, reached Paris after his expulsion in December 1968, he declared: "We shall continue to fight for regional freedom and for free syndicates and political associations." But after the expulsion of their "king", the Carlists divided into an anti-government majority and a pro-Franco minority. Some of their older notables were to be found in the government, but with each successive cabinet their number declined. Today, the Carlist community, still quite strong and vital in some districts of the north, has to counted among the forces opposed to and critical of the regime.

The Aperturistas

On the outer fringe of the establishment, but still belonging to it, one can discover these days a category of people, rather than a grouping or family, who have gained for themselves the name of *aperturistas*—those who advocate an opening up of the rather closed Spanish political system. They are not a family, because the aperturistas come historically from various backgrounds. They have no meeting-place, no newspaper or other periodical; each one fights his political crusade on his own. What they have in common is the view that it is possible to democratize the Spanish political system without threatening its existence. This, they believe, can and should be done by developing the Spanish fundamental laws and their latent possibilities. They take as their starting-point certain passages such as the famous one in the *Ley Orgánica,* the Organic Law, which declares that it is one of tasks of the National Movement to foster the participation of the people in politics and to encourage a contrast of opinions among them.

They insist on the need to procure the cooperation of the Spaniards with the regime for its own good and, indeed, for its very stability, particularly in anticipation of the time when "Franco will not be with us any more." Their fundamental thesis is that a system ought to be built today, before Franco dies, which would give the regime a broad base—provided chiefly by the new middle classes and the circles allied to them, whose interests demand gradual change and stability, and who fear nothing more than a renewed Civil War after Franco. The aperturistas believe that such center groupings, if they could only exist and act legally, would constitute the best guarantee for the permanence of the regime. They argue that by a judicious interpretation of the present fundamental laws, political conditions could be created which would permit the new middle classes to have a voice in the running of the country. Their principal legal difficulty seems to be the fact that the Spanish political system, as it is at present, has a certain coherence. The people of the old political school, Falangists and conservatives and, it would seem, Franco himself, argue that the essence of the regime cannot be altered. They regard certain proscriptions as being of its very core: the prohibition of political parties; the prohibition of the popular vote; the prohibition of free syndicates. These are things that would appear to be equally essential for any reformed regime that was to mobilize a considerable amount of middle-class and popular support for itself. The intransigent Falangists and supporters of the regime, with Franco's backing, it would appear, have so far been able to block any attempts by the aperturistas to achieve a real transformation.

In January 1974, the new government of Arias Navarro made some explicit promises of an opening of the political order. This was to consist of four important changes. Navarro promised that the *alcaldes* (mayors) would in future be elected. (He did not say by whom, and he might well have been thinking in terms of the Spanish system of electoral colleges: one consisting, say, of the *consejales*—municipal and other councillors.) Another promise was that in future there would be a greater separation of powers in the Cortes. This was to be achieved by a "law of incompatibilities", which would prohibit a person from being both a deputy in the Cortes and a member of the administration or the upper bureaucracy. Today, the majority of the deputies are linked closely to the administration. The real significance of a law on this matter will depend on the degree of exclusiveness it imposes. The prime minister also promised some kind of liberty of association within the state syndicates and the famous political associations. But he gave no indication as to how these measures would be legislated, and the degree of real freedom the eventual laws will permit is still a matter to be revealed.

But the mere declarations of the new government gave the aperturistas a chance to speak their minds publicly. They cannot be accused, as has happened in the past, of wanting to subvert the regime when they speak of and discuss reforms which the government itself says it wants to institute.

Who are the aperturistas within the Spanish power structure? The weekly journal *Mundo,* in its issue of November 17, 1973, asked a number of prominent political commentators to name the 10 men in the regime most inclined towards "opening up". Somewhat surprisingly, Fraga Iribarne, the former Minister of Information and present ambassador in London, came out on top of the list. From the comments made by the people questioned, it appeared that Iribarne's press law was judged by the majority as the most outstanding achievement of aperturismo so far, notwithstanding its obvious limitations and weaknesses. As Minister of Information, Fraga Iribarne had been a hard authoritarian, possibly under pressure from his ministerial colleagues and Franco himself, and the political commentators were well aware of his record. But many of them seemed to be ready to give him considerable credit for his various declarations after his dismissal from the post in 1969. These are indeed very aperturist, as can be seen from one quoted by *Mundo* itself:

> "The basis of political evolution is the fact that such evolution must come from society itself. Society cannot be active and passive at the same time. To modernize, one must broaden participation. . . . If a political program of participation is to be attempted, it is obvious that the fundamental points are freedom of information and association."

This is typical of many of Iribarne's statements. It also serves to illustrate the measure of tolerance enjoyed by the aperturistas. A statement of this kind, made by someone who cannot be suspected of subversion—he is after all, an ex-minister,—may be called daring, but it is tolerated. It did not prevent Iribarne from being appointed an ambassador. But the statements always have to be couched in abstract terms, taking care that the language is juridical rather than political in flavor. If they became slightly more concrete than the example that has been given—for instance, contrasting the desired freedoms with the present restrictive situation—they would probably overstep the permissible limits.

Another liberal *aperturista* mentioned frequently by the commentators questioned by *Mundo* was José María de Areilza, formerly ambassador in Paris and Washington, and one of the advocates of a more "European" policy, both domestically and externally. But it may not be altogether correct to count Areilza as belonging to the regime. He might well have become prime minister if Don Juan had become king; he belonged to the Conde de Barcelona's now dissolved "privy council". Today, perhaps, he should be placed in the right wing of the opposition rather than on the liberal wing of the regime. He was once fined for attempting, together with some other politicians of the moderate opposition, to contact a visiting U.S. statesman in order to draw his attention to the less democratic aspects of the regime.

A name mentioned by many of the commentators was that of another man in the same category, Joaquín Ruiz-Giménez, an ex-Minister of Education dismissed in 1956, today the moving spirit of the monthly *Cuadernos para el Diálogo,* which has become a platform for liberals, Christian Democrats, and, perhaps most of all, left Catholics. Ruiz-Giménez (also spelled Jiménez) belongs even less to the regime and more to the opposition then Areilza.

Two personalities closer to the government also figured near the top of the list: Cantarero del Castillo and Orti Bordas. Both are lawyers, both have come up through the SEU, and both are young by Spanish standards.

Canterero del Castillo, whose last book was entitled "Falange and Socialism", is the driving force behind the grouping of former members of the SEU, the university syndicate. Their weekly, *Criba* (which has now ceased publication, apparently for lack of funds) called consistently for the democratization of the regime—for "the democratic rationalization of the political and social structures of Spain", to use one of del Castillo's favorite phrases.

Orti Bordas has been through the administration to reach its top ranks. He has held such leading positions as: head of the information and press department of the Ministry of Information;

director of study projects in the now defunct SEU; president of that syndicate in 1964; inspector of associations in the Movimiento, and its deputy secretary-general until 1972. He sits on the National Council as member for the province of Castellón. Bordas has always spoken out for a democratic opening of the political structures of the country and continues to advocate them in the press.

Another aperturista lawyer, this one a member of the present government, is Martínez Esteruelas. In the past he has served as head of the legal office of the Movement and as director of the educational and scientific institution, the Juan March Foundation. He is the author of a book entitled "Political Enmity." In 1973 he succeeded López Rodó in the sensitive economic position of Minister of Planning and Development; but after the assassination of Carrero Blanco he was moved to the chaotic Ministry of Education. This portfolio is one of the most difficult in the whole government, and one that can either make or break a man. Shortly after assuming his new position, Martínez Esteruelas gave evidence that he still maintained his aperturist views when he declared in a speech at the state-controlled Institute of Political Studies: "The play of legitimate interests is no longer enough; it must give way to the play of opinions."

Among the popular names on the *Mundo* list was that of general Manuel Diez-Alegría, the chief of staff, who belongs to the intellectual minority of the army. Before becoming chief of staff he was director of the Higher Institute of National Defense. Diez-Alegría has made his liberal opinions heard in the Cortes, of which he is an ex-officio member, particularly on the controversial problem of what to do with conscientious objectors. But he has not succeeded in getting his views on this question accepted.

Jesus Esperabé de Arteaga, whose name was given by many of those questioned by *Mundo,* is one of the most outstanding liberals in the Cortes, where he sits as a "family representative" for the province of Salamanca. These family representatives are the only deputies elected by anything approaching a popular vote: two are elected in each of Spain's 50 provinces by heads of families and married women. Esperabé de Arteaga's activities, though energetic, are limited in scope; he confines himself to general statements, occasional questions to the government, and contacts with the press. He has very few supporters in the Cortes.

There are several ex-ministers whom the commentators canvassed by *Mundo* adjudged to be aperturistas. López Bravo, one of the key men of the Opus, served terms as Minister of Commerce and Minister of Foreign Affairs between 1962 and 1973. Villar Palasí was Minister of Education from 1968 and 1973, during which time he initiated, but was unable to complete, a massive program of educational reform. Solís Ruiz, a clever speaker and a juggler with words and concepts, was Minister and Secretary-General of the *Movimiento* from 1957 to 1969. As such he was in charge of the syndicates. He did what he could to liberalize them, but it was not very much. Castiella, who was at the Foreign Ministry from 1957 to 1969, can be called an aperturista because of his attempts to "open" Spain toward the Common Market and—on the consular level only—toward the Communist bloc countries. But in earlier times he wrote some fairly hair-raising Falangist prose about the Spanish Empire. Silva Muñoz, Minister of Public Works from 1965 to 1970, is a member of *Acción Catolica* and the leading man in the traditional Church sector whose opinions are given public airing in the daily newspaper *Ya*. Munoz has a reputation as a quiet and efficient organizer. Not without ambition, he is regarded as someone who may have a big political career ahead of him.

Bourgeois Democrats

On the other side of the political equator which separates the Spanish establishment from the opposition, but close to the dividing line, there are a number of moderate opposition politicians who, because of their personal distinction, are allowed some kind of semi-legal existence but who are not permitted to organize any groups or parties around themselves. The Christian democrats have their journals, and around these they are able to mobilize a few people; but the democratic socialists do not have any, presumably because they have never been able to obtain permits to publish them. An attempt is underway to start a big liberal national daily newspaper. A company has been founded; shares have been sold; a building has been acquired; an editor has been nominated. If *El Pais* ("The Country") ever starts publication, it could serve as a wider rallying ground for democratic liberal, democratic socialist, and Christian democratic tendencies. But it is this very fact, one suspects, that has held up the grant of the necessary permit. All these tendencies are outlawed in Spain, and any dissemination of them would, technically speaking, constitute the crime of "illegal propaganda" and render the perpetrators liable to prosecution by a *tribunal de orden público.*

These public order courts are an essential feature of the Spanish political scene. They were established in June 1959 when the "Order Law" was enacted. Under their special procedure, the judges may accept a written accusation by the police as proof of an established fact. In theory the trials are public, but many of them proceed without the public being aware of the substance of the accusation, because the judges rely on written evidence proffered in court. In most cases, only such points as the defense lawyers raise get any public mention.

Under these conditions the bourgeois opposition in Spain has generally kept silent. It is fragmented and disorganized. It has, after all, lived for more than a generation (practically since 1936) without any possibility of political action, except underground. There have been a few instances of bourgeois opposition initiative, probably the most recent one—and the only one with any permanent effect—being the congress at Munich in 1962, at which 80 prominent Spaniards met with 38 of their exiled countrymen. The outcome of the congress was a manifesto calling on the nations of the European Economic Community not to admit Spain to membership until the regime had been liberalized. Five concrete points were mentioned: true democratic representation and a government based on the consent of the governed; human rights, especially those of free assembly and speech and an end to censorship; recognition of the diversity of the different ethnic minorities of Spain, such as Basques, Catalans, Gallegos; genuinely free syndicates and freedom to strike; acknowledgement of the right to hold political opinions, and to form political parties and a legal opposition.

The 80 representatives from Spain were led by the veteran parliamentarian Gil Robles, who had been the leader of the right-of-center Catholic bloc (CEDA) before the Civil War. The exiles were led by Rodolfo Llopis, the leader of Spanish Socialism in exile, who lived in France. Salvador de Madariaga, the exiled Spanish writer and liberal politician who lives in England, was mainly responsible for organizing the congress—and a hard job it was for him. Most of the participants from Spain were punished when they returned home. Gil Robles was given the choice of exile or banishment to Spain's Canary Islands. He chose exile. The liberal politicans. Satrústegui and Álvarez de Miranda went to the Canaries. The poet and Falangist-turned-liberal, Dionisio Ridruejo, did not return with the others; he stayed abroad for two years in France and Italy, and finally returned secretly to Spain, where he was imprisoned for a few years and then released on condition that he remain quiet.

The two monthlies published by the Christian opposition are *DC* and *Cuadernos para el Diálogo. DC* officially stands for *Diálogo y Convivencia,* but the periodical likes to use only the initials, which are also those of *Democracia Cristiana.* It is published by the deputy editor of the Catholic conservative daily *Ya,* Luis Apostua. Every issue contains news about the Christian democratic movements in Italy, South America, Germany, etc., thus making it clear that it considers itself the mouthpiece of this political trend even though it cannot proclaim so openly. Most of its other articles are of a political character. They tend to be critical of the regime—but are always careful to maintain the proper respect which is legally imperative—and to call for its democratization.

Cuadernos para el Diálogo is much the larger of the two journals and one of the most influential periodicals in the country. In order to increase its total volume, it publishes a number of supplements every year in addition to its monthly issues. The founder of the review was Joaquín Ruiz-Jiménez, the Minister of Education dismissed in 1957. He cannot figure as the editor because of legal complications: under the press law, an editor has to have a diploma in journalism from the state school of journalism. But most of the editorials appearing anonymously in the review are from his pen. Over the long period of his opposition, Ruiz-Jiménez, a personal friend of the Pope, has gradually veered to the left. His periodical represents the views of the left Catholics, all the way from slightly left of the Pope to the Catholic Marxists and an occasional Marxist minus the Catholicism.

Cuadernos, which operates under constant threat of fines and confiscation, publishes some of the most rewarding commentary on the political scene, and articles on political and social questions, to be found in Spain. The supplements, which are often monographs on one specific subject, are also of great value and importance. If parties were allowed, the people around *Cuadernos* would probably form something in the nature of a Christian Socialist political group. But they have no chance of becoming politically active except on the intellectual level through their review and the books put out by the publishing company *Cuadernos* owns.

A few degrees to the left of *Cuadernos* there are several Church publications aimed at a wide readership and defending the views of the progressive Catholics; they are mostly Jesuit-inspired. The most outstanding are *Mundo Social* and *Hechos y Dichos.* Both have a long history of fines, confiscation, and interference by the information authorities. Unfortunately, both are rather expensive for reviews intended for a large Spanish public, and finance, particularly in view of the losses caused by fines and seizures, is bound to be a great problem.

The universities are another focal point of bourgeois opposition. The students—if they are politically active at all—tend to stand to the left, but the teaching staff nearly always includes a considerable number of fairly liberal intellectuals critical of the regime. Their possibilities of political action are minimal. The fact that the student body is inclined to get involved in unruly disputes, sometimes leading to violence, while they—the faculty— are in theory responsible for the behavior of the students, puts them into a difficult position. University officials, up to the rank of Dean, used to be elected by their colleagues; rectors have always been nominated by the authorities. But a reorganization carried out in 1973 gave the Ministry of Education the power to nominate all university officials and at the same time made the latter responsible for the discipline and good behavior of the students, particularly in the field of politics. The state of the universities is best described as intermittent chaos. University teachers, if they mix in politics at all, are mostly caught up in this peculiar chaos of university politics, which will be described later.

There is also a Spanish Socialist Party, which aims at democratic socialism and is in contact with the Socialist parties of Europe. Its visible head is the lawyer Tierno Galván, who was dismissed from the University of Salamanca in 1965 and who tries to keep alive what has been called "University Socialism" among teachers and students.

Workers' Commissions

The workers' commissions—*comisiones obreras*—that first made their appearance during the strikes of 1956-57, were one of the many significant phenomena of a year that can be regarded as a turning-point in recent Spanish history. They were the spontaneous creation of the workers, produced in response to the restrictiveness of sindicatos. The workers knew they could not trust their official delegates to represent their true interests in negotiations with the employers, especially once a strike had begun. In fact, it is at the very moment a strike breaks out that the true nature of the official syndicate hierarchy becomes clear. Their primary task is not to help the workers but to end the strike, by all possible means, including denunciation of the strike leaders to the police.

Once the strike has been broken and the leaders have been arrested, the official delegates return to their role of representing the workers; they may even negotiate a settlement somewhat less disadvantageous to the workers than the previous arrangement. Their principal political task is to keep the workers' movement under control. If such control is better served by some modest concessions, they may agree to these or allow themselves to be pressured into accepting them. But they cannot and will not permit free play of the opposing social forces, employees and employers. If they did, they would lose their usefulness to the regime and, consequently, their jobs.

It was this past experience with their official representatives that induced the workers to nominate or elect responsible groups from their own ranks to lead strikes and negotiate settlements. At first the function of the comisiones obreras was limited to a specific negotiation or strike; but once they were established the nature of their work tended to keep them as a permanent institution. There were always problems to be settled, agreements to be followed up, and future negotiations to be prepared. But by reason of their origin, the commissions have remained subject to strict control by the workers. A workers' meeting can remove any member at any time if a majority decides that it has lost confidence in him as a representative.

The big strikes of 1962 and 1963, mainly in Asturias, the Basque provinces, Catalonia, and Madrid, turned the comisiones into a kind of national movement. Militant workers of all different political colors tried to get onto the committees. There were moments when the official syndicate hierarchy found itself forced to deal with the workers' commission directly, so dangerous had the strikes become. Solis, the sindicatos minister, seemed for a time prepared to accept a dialogue. Perhaps he hoped sincerely to bring the new militants into the official structures; but it may be that right from the start he and his services aimed only at gaining access to information in order to bring their political *fichiers*—their records—up to date so that they could make arrests when the time was ripe. Whatever the original intention, the contacts of the syndicates and their bosses with the comisiones were eventually used for the repression of the leaders. The power of the workers' commissions reached its peak towards the winter of 1967, when the strike of the Madrid metal workers forced the judges of the public order tribunal to liberate the comisiones leader, Camacho, and send him to the factories by car in order to calm down the workers.

The big crackdown followed in 1967 and 1968. The police proved to be so well informed about the varied mass activities of the commissions that it was obvious that they had planted stool pigeons in the factories. Whenever workers held a meeting—which was often done in the open, close to the plant—police turned up, surrounded them and took away the leaders or those who were alleged to be the leaders. Often the men of the *brigada social* (political police) knew before the action started whom they were looking for.

Parallel with these police activities, the public order tribunals evolved a doctrine which regarded the comisiones as organs of the Communist Party. This was "proved" with the help of books such as "After Franco, What?" by the exiled Communist Party chief, Santiago Carrillo. In writings like these one does in fact find references to the comisiones movement as "our action" and "our mass movement"; but one also finds other passages which make it clear that, according to Carrillo, it is necessary to cooperate with any force opposed to Franco. Consider the following statement:

> "It is true that in general it is we [i.e., the Communists] who furnish the political line and the correct solutions. But this role will be all the more effective, more real, more complete, if we know how to integrate into our line, and without mental reservations, the judgments and opinions of other groups. This means that in practise we have to achieve a synthesis of our own initiatives and those which may come from other groups." [S. Carrillo: *Despois de Franco . . . o qué? Compasso do tempo,* Lisbon s.a. p. 58. First published in French in 1966. The Spanish edition is not available to the writer.]

Whatever may be the real composition of political groups in the comisiones, or more generally of groups that put forward demands as far as the public order tribunals are concerned they are all sub-organizations of the Spanish Communist Party. This has been confirmed by the *Supremo*, the highest court of appeal, and has become judicial doctrine. In fact there is little doubt that Communist workers play an important part in the commissions; but they also include many leftist Christians and—with certain variations according to the region—the militants of the Socialists in exile (directed from Toulouse) and of Catalan and Basque Socialism. Even elements of the left Falange groups are not lacking.

It is relatively easy for the comisiones to form committees at the factory-floor level. But as soon as several factories try to coordinate their activities—and, even more so if an attempt is made to coordinate industrial action on an urban, provincial or national level—the police do their very best to intervene and put a stop to it. The reasons for this are clear. Local strikes can achieve certain limited local demands, more pay, and better working conditions; but the basic political demands of the movement can only be achieved by a widespread, if possible nationwide, strike movement. The main political demands of the comisiones have always been for liberty to strike, liberty to organize, the freeing of political prisoners, freedom of assembly, freedom of speech and writing, and free political parties. The specific freedoms of labor have, naturally, been closest to their hearts.

It is against the political demands of the movement that the state has mobilized all its resources. The specialized brigada social, in collaboration with the official syndicates and using all kinds of techniques for infiltrating the factories and workers commissions, is intent above all upon disrupting communication. Only by communication, written or verbal, meetings, conventions, and so on, can the commissions hope to coordinate their actions to such a degree that a widespread movement, with political impact, becomes possible. That is why all the prohibitions—e.g., of assembly, of publication—are so strictly imposed in the labor field. Workers' delegates, even if elected within the framework of the official syndicates, are not allowed to assemble except under the supervision of their president, who is an officer imposed by the state hierarchy. He is responsible for ensuring that nothing is discussed except what is on the agenda, which has to be approved in advance by the hierarchy.

In view of these severe restrictions, the leaders of the comisiones have taken in many cases to assembling in churches or church premises. These, under the 1953 Concordat, are immune from intrusion by the police. There were some years, roughly between 1967 and 1970, when the police were in the habit of surrounding the churches and asking workers to identify themselves as they came out. But later a more effective method was devised. Groups of Falangist extremists were encouraged by the police to break into the churches and to set upon the people assembled therein. Many of the bravoes were armed. Not long ago in a Madrid bank-robbery trial the possession of revolvers by the accused, who were members of the extreme right wing, was explained by the fact that some had been licensed to leaders of the political group who were engaged in assisting certain auxiliary forces of order against "red subversion" (see *Informaciones,* Madrid, February 8, 1974 *Juicio del TOP contra cuatro miembros de "Cruz Ibérica"*). Some of the priests involved in the use of churches by the workers were themselves sent to prison on various pretexts.

In the years after 1970 there was increasing criticism of the comisiones by left-wing groups, who were disappointed at what seemed to them the stagnation, or even the decline, of the movement. The leftist critics saw the principal reason for this as the too-overt tactics of the commissions. They had attempted to work in a semi-legal manner, and they had made it easy for the police to clamp down on them. The critics began to think that their main mistake was to have underestimated the seriousness and determination of the regime, and of the police and their readiness to suppress the commissions ruthlessly.

It is probably still true today that the comisiones are the most prominent, the largest, and the most widespread movement of resistance to the regime. The workers are constantly provoked to resist by what they see as the obvious injustice of the state syndicates. But the comisiones do not have enough cohesion and coordination to foment any politically decisive strike action. In the last few years they have even given up trying to call for days of mass demonstrations and strikes as they had done, with limited success, up to 1969, on the first of May or on other dates publicized in advance by a leaflet campaign. The biggest actions of recent years have been the well-nigh general strikes at Vigo in September 1972 and at Pamplona in May and June 1973. Both were limited to a single industrial region, even though in both cases there were some solidarity strikes in Catalonia. Essentially they represented the upper limit of extent and intensity that can be achieved by a movement when the local organizations on the factory-floors exist, but when no nationwide planning and no large-scale agitation are possible. In both Vigo and Pamplona, the circumstances were such that widespread solidarity strikes could be whipped up in and around an industrial center surrounded by a more or less apathetic countryside. In both cases the settlements were relatively favorable for the workers, but some of the more important strike leaders were arrested and lost their jobs, if not their freedom. Another important strike with similar characteristics—a local stoppage paralyzing one town and industrial region for a fairly extended period—took place in El Ferrol in the spring of 1972.

The sympathizers of the comisiones defend themselves against the attacks of the left extremists, such as FRAP (discussed below) and PCE (the Communist Party), by pointing to the mobile nature of the Spanish working class. In the newer industrial centers, the worker comes straight from the country and has no conception of workers' organizations. The leaders of the comisiones movement are of the opinion that for the time being there is no scope for activity beyond what the local commissions are doing in the way of making demands on behalf of the workers they represent.

> "The rejection by the working-class world of all the secret organizations has been interpreted by the political elements as the apolitical attitude of the working class, but it seems rather to indicate a clear awareness of its real situation in Spain and its true possibilities of action. What is usually called a strong class conscience."

So write two of the pro-commission militants, E. and A. López Campillo, in an article entitled *La stratégie des commissions ouvrières* in *Le Monde Diplomatique* of February, 1974. In the same issue, a voice close to the Maoists speaks of the "decline of the commissions" and believes that the revolutionary actions of the more radical minorities represent the wave of the future (Jaime Martín, *Une nouvelle etappe de la lutte populaire*).

The last public event centering in the comisiones was Trial 1001, in which ten persons were accused by the Madrid public order court of being the principal leaders of the comisiones, and were found guilty of the charge. They had been arrested on June 24, 1972, in and around the monastery of the Padres Oblatos at Pozuelo de Alarión, a suburb of the capital. The trial took place on December 20, 1973, and on succeeding days under the shadow of the assassination of Prime Minister Carrero Blanco, which occurred, apparently by chance, on the day it opened.

The accusation seems to have been that the ten men were top leaders of the comisiones obreras and had come to the monastery for a meeting. They did, it is true, hail from different provinces. The arrests had been made by motorized police who surrounded the monastery. They had told the inhabitants of the village, presumably in order to get their cooperation, that they were after a dope ring. At the trial, the prosecution called no witnesses. Reporting was sketchy; only a few news agencies were admitted to witness the proceedings—the three official and the one unofficial Spanish agencies and some of the big international press services. The defense was led by some of Spain's leading lawyers. Ruiz-Jiménez represented the most prominent of the accused, the 55-year-old metal worker Marcelino Camacho, formerly a workers' representative (*enlace*) at Perkins Ibérica and one of the best-known labor leaders in the country. He had previous convictions for illegal demonstration, illicit association, and contempt of court, and except for three-and-a-half-months in 1972 he had been in prison since January 1967.

The other nine accused were:

(1) Nicolas Sartorius, lawyer and journalist, previously convicted of "military rebellion" and "non-peaceful assembly". "Military rebellion" was the blanket crime of which all military and civilian supporters of the Republican government, many of them recruited by force, could be accused after the Civil War;

(2) Eduardo Saborido Galán from Seville, formerly a workers' representative in the metal section in that city, previously convicted of illicit association and non-peaceful demonstration;

(3) Fernando Soto Martino, metal worker from Seville, previously convicted of non-peaceful demonstration;

(4) Francisco Acosta Orga, mechanic and taxi driver, with no criminal record;

(5) Miguel Angel Zamora Antón from Saragossa, worker in the butane gas industry, with no criminal record;

(6) Pedro Santiestebán Hurtado from Vizcaya, worker, with no criminal record;

(7) Juan Marcos Muñiz Zapico from Valladolid, electrician, with no criminal record;

(8) Francisco García Salve, 43, worker priest, previously convicted by the public order courts and several trials pending; and

(9) Luis Fernández Costilla from Valladolid.

All denied the accusation, giving various explanations for their presence at the monastery. But the tribunal, for its own reasons—which were not published—disbelieved them. Sentences were pronounced on December 27 and published two days later. They were very severe: 28 years' imprisonment for Camacho; 20 years and six months for Saborido; 19 years for Sartorius and García Salve; 18 years for Muñiz Zapico; 17 years and four months for Soto Martín, and 12 years for Acosta Orga and the rest. Foreign observers were principally concerned with the lack of formal proof and the long delay—18 months—between the arrest and trial of the accused. Appeals before the Supreme Court were still pending at the time of writing.

There is little doubt that the workers' commissions are an important instrument of fomentation among the Spanish workers. Many of their leaders see their activity as a kind of pedogagical effort, aimed at maintaining the spirit of struggle and combativeness among the workers, and they intend to foster this by gaining small but significant successes in the areas of wages and working conditions. They hope that these will help the workers, many of them newly arrived from rural areas, to recognize the value of association and self-help.

The drawback of this strategy is that the government makes the leaders pay for their initiative by imprisonment and dismissal from work, which often results in their having to emigrate. Thus each gain by strike action has to be paid for by a more or less complete decapitation of the leadership. In practice, it is almost impossible to lead a strike without becoming known to the brigada social. All this is compounded by inflation. Rising prices give the workers the feeling, in many respects justified, that they have to keep running (including risking illegal strikes) in order to stay in the same place. And this running has to be paid for by the punishment and removal of each successive generation of emergent leaders.

In the existing circumstances, one of the main questions one has to ask about the commissions is: how long will it be until relatively mild and nonviolent organs are reduced by repression to such a state that they either modify their methods or make way for new, more violent, more politically oriented, and more radically revolutionary illegal groupings? It would appear that both developments have already begun, and one must envisage that they will continue to grow. The degree of radicalization will depend on such imponderables as the general state of the economy (growth will reduce it, stagnation or recession foster it strongly); the rate of inflation; a mass return of Spanish workers from other countries in Europe; the level of employment; and the ferocity or relative leniency of repression. At the time of writing, the outlook in most of these matters is less favorable than in earlier years. Already there is talk of the comisiones obreras revising their strategy and tactics and forming smaller, more secretive, and more activist cells. On the other hand, there are increasing attempts by extremist radical groups to the left of the commissions to outbid them in what they have to offer to the workers.

The Communist Party

In many respects the *Partido Communista de España* (PCE), the Communist Party of Spain, is *the* opposition party. There must be many Spaniards who have no idea, or at least no clear idea, what the bourgeois opposition groups—the Liberals, the Democractic Christians, the Democratic Socialists, etc.—are and what they want. This is only natural, for these groups have no legal way of making themselves widely known; legally, they do not even exist. But there can be few Spaniards who do not know who the Communists are, or who have no idea of what they want. The Communists are the only opposition group which has a solid clandestine party network. They claim to have about 100,000 supporters in the country, perhaps half of them party members. If one counts their families, one arrives at a figure of roughly 350,000 people likely to be in some kind of contact with the party. Nobody knows for sure whether those numbers are inflated or not, not even the security authorities.

The position of the Communists as the only solid nucleus of opposition to the regime entails for them both an advantage and a drawback. The advantage is that people who are really serious about opposing the regime will nearly always gravitate towards the Communists, for they are the only serious group active. Witnesses to the gravitational attraction of the PCE are the left Christians, who have grown so progressively closer to the Communist Party that in many cases their positions are almost indistinguishable, notwithstanding their strong reservations on religious grounds. The comisiones have also felt the pull of the Communist Party. Certainly in the eyes of the government they are nothing but a dependency of the PCE. This is probably an exaggeration, but there is little doubt that the party helps to formulate their policies and that it has been furnishing leaders of the commissions which, on the other hand, the Party has managed to use as recruiting grounds.

The disadvantage to the Communists in being the only real and active center of opposition to the regime arises from circumstances in which many Spaniards who dislike the regime distrust the Communists even more. These groups or individuals tend to remain inactive because they do not want to collaborate with or serve the interests of the PCE. Their attitude has to be seen in the light of the past. The power struggles around the PCE during the Civil War were very vicious, going so far that in Barcelona there took place a revolution within the revolution, which featured the famous crushing of the dissident left of the Barcelona POUM in May 1937 and the persecution, torture and murder of the POUM leaders by Chekas of Soviet specialists.

It is the regime which has profited time and again from the past sins of the Communists. Antipathy to them is very strong among both bourgeoisie and the peasants, who have often reached the conclusion that they would rather have Franco than the Communists. They have discerned no midway point between these extremes; and the fact that in practical terms many people see a categorical choice between two unattractive alternatives has reinforced a traditional tendency to look on politics as something basically evil, dishonest, and best steered clear of. This attitude prevails in the Spanish provinces to this day.

The Spanish Communists, under their present leader, Santiago Carrillo, have become aware of their basic strength and their basic weakness, and have evolved a policy which takes both into account. The basic strength being a type of monopoly in organization inside the Spanish opposition, their weakness a brand of isolation to which they are exposed by means of their past and their Communist label, the PCE has gone all out to change its image.

From 1966 onwards, the PCE has been calling for a grand alliance of all anti-Franco forces, "Even those whose aims are opposed to ours and who have in the past aided the Franquist regime" (to quote Santiago Carrillo in an interview with *Le Monde,* November 4, 1970). This is the "Alliance for Freedom," the main platform of the CP. It has been achieved, at least in theory, in Catalonia; but in Madrid, the bourgeois forces and even the Democratic Socialists have so far resisted the blandishments of the Communists.

In November 1971, about 300 people managed to gather in a Barcelona church without the police finding out. They called themselves the first assembly of the democratic forces of Catalonia, and they adopted a four-point program: an amnesty for prisoners and exiles; exercise of democractic freedoms and rights; re-establishment of Catalan autonomy in accordance with the law of 1932 as a first step toward self-determination for all the peoples of Spain; and coordination of the democratic forces in their fight to achieve these aims. The meeting, which lasted five hours, elected a permanent commission to follow up the decisions. It had been prepared during the whole of the preceding year by a coordinating commission which included the Catalan Republican Left (*Esquerra republicana*), the Catalan Socialist Movement, the Catalan Democratic Union, the Catalan United Socialist Party (which is the name of the Catalan PC), and the Catalan National Front. In the assembly there were also delegates of the workers' movement, the comisiones obreras, and the UGT, the Socialist trade union. A number of representatives of the bourgeoisie also took part as individuals. The monarchist supporters of Don Juan could not accept the third point of the program (about Catalan autonomy), but they did approve the others.

Two years later, on October 28, 1973, another group of 113 people gathered in a church of Barcelona, but were surprised by the police and arrested. They were accused of being the preparatory committee gathered to prepare a second assembly of the democratic forces of Catalonia. Some of the participants were set free with a caution after a few days; others were kept in prison. Among the latter were no doubt the people suspected by the police of belonging to the Communists, the comisiones, and other organizations they considered especially dangerous. All 113 were to go before the public order courts. It would appear that the second democratic assembly was infiltrated by the police and denounced.

In the two years between the two assemblies, the "democratic forces" do not seem to have achieved many practical results. The present writer, who lives in Madrid, did not hear any talk of activities in the capital except for an attempt at a similar assembly which was unsuccessful. The Madrid political groups were too suspicious of the Communists, who were seen as the prime movers of the scheme, to participate. In Catalonia circumstances had been different, because in addition to the dislike of the regime there was also the common bond of Catalan national feeling to draw the opposition together.

The PCE continues its efforts to coordinate and activate a broad democratic front. It is certainly no accident that in pursuing this aim, it has gone about as far to the right as is possible for a Communist party.

Carrillo said in his *Le Monde* interview that he could very well envisage a Socialist Spain "where the prime minister would be a Catholic and the Communist Party would be a minority." In this democratic approach, the Spanish Communists have much in common with the Italian party. Indeed, they are generally said to stand even further to the right. It is not surprising that their democratic line has led them into trouble with Moscow. They protested violently, as did many other European Communist parties, against the Soviet intervention in Czechoslovakia in 1968. The plenary reunion of their executive voted 66 to five against that intervention. Two of the pro-Moscow minority leaders, Eduardo García and Augustín Gómez, were thrown out of the party in 1969. Enrique Lister, the successful general on the Republican side in the Civil War, took up their defense and he, too, was finally expelled in September 1970. Four members of the central committee followed him: Barzana, Balague, Saiz, and Uriarte. Two separate editions of the party paper began to appear, both under the original name, *Mundo Obrero.* The *Mundo Obréro* of the Lister minority, which follows the Moscow line, has a red masthead; the mouthpiece of Santiago Carrillo bears a black one. The journal is usually printed in France on thin paper and smuggled into Spain, where it is not easy to come by. Many Spaniards learn about its contents from the broadcasting station that identifies itself as "*Radio Pirenaica,* the only Spanish station without Franco's censorship." Its transmitters are said to be actually located in Sofia, and the programs, according to well-informed exiles, are produced in Prague. It is beamed to Spain by shortwave, and the Spanish authorities try to obstruct it. The interference is quite effective in the center of the big towns, but in the outskirts and industrial suburbs the station is clearly audible. By following it regularly one can obtain a fairly complete picture of the party line which, at least so far, has remained the Carrillo line.

As far as Spain is concerned, the majority of Carrillo's faction wants to work toward a gradual liberalization and democratization, using their own strength and political activity and mobilizing a maximum of aid from all democratic circles. The Lister minority seems to rely, rather, on extraordinary circumstances such as a breakdown of European prosperity or even a major war, in order to change the political climate in their favor. There is little doubt that by far the larger part of Carrillo's followers can be found in Spain itself; the Lister adherents are mainly in exile. But according to Carrillo himself, even among the 1,000-odd Spaniards living in the Soviet Union, 900 go along with him, while in France there are only about 60 Lister adherents among the more than 10,000 exiled Spanish Communists living there. Most of these claims must be true, because it would otherwise be impossible to explain how the Carrillo faction continues to dominate the official party even in places like Prague, Sofia, and Moscow.

This was not the only split the PCE suffered. A few years earlier, in 1964, the Maoist-Leninist faction had broken away and founded their own group, referred to from now on as PCE (M-l). In 1966 there was another rupture, this time engineered by Claudin, who began airing his opposition to Carrillo in *Ruedo Ibérica,* a periodical put out by a Paris publishing house of the same name. Claudin, too, criticized Carrillo for not being sufficiently to the left. What he wanted was a revolution in Spain; he did not believe in tactical collaboration with the bourgeoisie. It was the old polemic that had raged at the time of the Civil War all over again: "Popular Front" versus "Revolution Now".

Since in the eyes of the immense majority of the population the Spanish Communists represent practically all opposition, they serve as a pole of attraction to those who feel themselves treated unjustly by the regime. The most important in these groups are the workers, who regard the sindicatos systems as an injustice imposed on them by the victors of the Civil War so that the latter can enjoy the fruits of victory by exploiting the working class. There is enough truth in this simplified view of things to turn most of the workers who think in political terms into secret or open rebels against the regime, and this politicized minority gravitates towards the CPE.

The great weaknesses of the party are its history, its foreign connections, and its inability—as far as one knows—to infiltrate the armed forces. The armed forces, maintaining the tradition of the Civil War, have remained violently hostile to all "reds". They have been taught to see themselves as Spain's bulwark against red subversion, and all the indications are that this mission is still very much alive in their midst. The real strength of the regime has always been the army and the armed police forces. As long as they remain solidly against the PCE, there seems to be very little chance for the party to bring off a successful revolution. Those Communists who—like Carrillo—recognize this situation, seek a way out of the impasse by association with other "democratic forces". Those other forces do have some influence in the army, and this fact alone may make it worthwhile for the PCE to cultivate their friendship.

The hard-line "revolutionaries" who split off from the PCE are basically persons not deeply concerned with the realities of power in Spain or in their analysis. They have a mystical belief in "the people" and in their capacity to launch, one day, the revolution that will achieve the transition to Socialism in a single step. These extremists dislike the idea of an alliance with the moderates and the democrats. They would rather have the people endure more and harsher suffering so that eventually, out of the depths of their despair, they will produce the revolution which—so the extremists fear—might otherwise be smothered by a soft, bourgeois, and neocapitalist evolution, corrupting the masses with the deceptive blessings of the consumer's society and all that it stands for. The slogan of these extremists is always "The worse the better"—meaning the worse things are, the better grow the prospects in the long run for the revolution.

This stance has basic flaws due to the position of the army. As long as a sharp division persists between the two Spains—the Spain of the revolutionaries and the Spain of order—the army and the armed police forces will always take their stand on the side of order. Only by blurring the dividing line and involving the two Spains in one common purpose can any basis of solidarity between worker and policeman, intellectual and officer, be established. Such a basis is the precondition for any successful change of regime. But the common purpose cannot be revolution: it must involve a goal recognized by everyone as leading toward and aiming at a freer, more prosperous society.

The Maoists

Although the Spanish Maoists split off from the PCE in 1964, not much was heard of them until the 1970s. They have consistently attacked PCE, and they call the comisiones a creation of Carrillo. In the last few years they have begun to emulate the tactics of the PCE by forming groups of sympathizers around the inner core of the party membership. There is a Marxist-Leninist peasants' movement; there are youth groups and womens' groups; there is an illegal syndicate, the OSO (*Oposición Sindical Obrera*); there are pro-FRAP committees; and finally there is the "United Front" which is supposed to embrace all these movements and groups—FRAP (*Frente Revolucionario Antifascista Popular*). FRAP gained a certain notoriety during 1973 even though it was only founded officially in January 1974; before that there had been, formally, only pro-FRAP committees.

One of the most frequent, and perhaps more pertinent, criticisms FRAP and the PCE (M-L) level against the comisiones and the PCE, but particularily the former, is that they work halfway in the open and are consequently exposed to sharp and ruinous blows of repression. As for themselves, they insist that they want to form very tightly knit revolutionary units with maximum security; consequently there is little information available about them. Their official voices are Radio Tirana in Spanish, easily received in Spain, and the illegal news bulletin of APEP (*Agencia de Prensa España Popular*), which appear in Spanish, French, German, and English. It is easily available in France, but difficult to obtain inside Spain. Radio Tirana and APEP contain roughly the same news. But the claims made in these official media are virtually impossible to check. Above all, it is very difficult to know how significant are the numbers of FRAP members.

The police communiqués, once arrests have been made, have supplied this much information: FRAP's main effort is in the direction of young people. Hardly any arrested member of FRAP or PCE (M-L) is over 25; on many occasions the victims have been groups of young workers, aged anywhere between 16 and 20, students, or even high-school pupils. There are several reasons for FRAP's special success with the young: it preaches an absolutist revolutionary doctrine without any compromises, which is something that has a particular appeal for young people. In their case it does not have to take into account a certain knowledge of the world and its ways and some experience of power. Adults possessed of this knowledge and experience are able to see through some of the more transparent pretensions and propaganda distortions of the Front. The young will be ready to believe in the feasibility of an abrupt revolution in Spain, while their elders may prove more sceptical. Even the abstract cruelty of "executing" a policeman may appeal to the young, who tend to forget that he is human as well and who, moreover, have probably never seen a man killed violently before.

Such an "execution" took place on May 1, 1973, close to the Madrid station of Atocha. According to FRAP, it was in retaliation for the shooting of a worker by Catalan police in San Adrian de los Besos, a suburb of Barcelona, in the previous month. One group of demonstrators provoked the police by carrying red banners. They ran away, followed by the police in a jeep, which was met by a second group armed with iron bars, hatchets and knives. One policeman was killed and two others were wounded. The police had strict orders not to use their arms. As a consequence of this act, which caused considerable commotion in Spain, 145 people were arrested and accused of belonging to FRAP. There were allegations that they were tortured and few people doubt those allegations, for the police were in a grim mood after the murder of their comrade.

The fury of the police manifested itself in street demonstrations by their own ranks, headed by the Falangist general and commander of the Guardia Civil, Iniesta Cana, and in the cry for rougher police methods and for the overthrow of the "soft" Opus Dei government. A few weeks later, in June, the government was changed and the Minister of the Interior, who had given the order not to use firearms on May 1, García Gonicaño, lost his job. After that date there was a considerable increase in the number of demonstrators shot "accidentally" by the police, or shot by them "in the course of duty". Some of these cases were publicized; others were hushed up. Naturally, a big police hunt was unleashed against FRAP, and it was started up again after the murder of Carrero Blanco in December 1973, even though this seemed to be the work of ETA—the Basque militants—and not of FRAP. The hunt was still proceeding at the time of this writing.

The political significance of this FRAP story is that the Communists are exposed by the existence of the Maoists to an "overbid" on their left. Rivalries between the two groups are so bitter that they work against each other, even in the prisons, each faction refusing participation in actions such as hunger strikes or protest movements when organized by its rival. Strike actions called for by the OSO have been known to be disavowed by comisiones, and the same is possibly true in reverse. There is little doubt that the left extremists will attempt one of their revolutionary actions in the event of Franco's death. What cannot be foreseen is the extent to which they will be able to summon people into the streets and create serious disturbances in the industrial cities. But it is quite clear that the more violent and effective their action, the more severe will be the reaction of the police and, if need be, the army. If there have been demonstrations by the police because of one dead policeman during the lifetime of Franco, one can imagine roughly what will happen in the case of a serious insurrectionary attempt after Franco has died, should the ultra-left prove to have anough strength to bring it off. It will be smashed, without any doubt; and if it is difficult to smash, matters will become much more serious. Troops may be called in—with the considerable danger that they will be loath to surrender their power after they have cleaned up the revolt.

All this must mean for the Communists (PCE) that they are no longer quite free to select their movements and actions according to their reading of the political situation in the country. They now must take into consideration that the PCE (M-L) might release an insurrection, which would face them with the alternative of either joining it or submitting to it without action and still risking subsequent repression. In other words, the PCE is no longer master of its tactical moves: it may have its hand forced by the ultra-left.

There is little doubt in the mind of this writer that any revolutionary or insurrectionary movement which takes to the streets now or in the near future will be smashed to bits by the police or, if necessary, by the army. There are many officers eager to do just that. There might be others who would see the suppression as a disagreeable duty, but they too would fulfill that duty as soon as it became evident that order was threatened. Order is the fetish of the armed forces in Spain, and they are not prepared to see it disrupted.

University Politics

University politics differ from ordinary politics because of the short time span of surveys or studies. They have to be reshaped with each generation of students and for this reason are rather like a merry-go-round. Students and professors are a special political public, more concerned with ideas and less with material issues than the average body politic. Finally, in university politics academic issues and questions of internal organization tend to become entwined with more ideological and political problems of concern to the community at large. In Spain, there is a clear technique of using university issues to obtain the involvement of the student masses, who cannot, at the start, be mobilized on purely political matters. In this respect, university politics resemble those of the comisiones; the activists try to involve the large masses, either of workers or of students, by bringing up issues that affect them all in their capacities as workers or students—industrial or academic working conditions.

Spanish university politics have been developing over a fairly long period, and, broadly speaking, they seem to have changed from a relatively clear-cut movement with fixed aims into something much more convulsive and chaotic. This is attributable partly to the operations of the repressive organs, the police, and the brigada social, which have succeeded in dismantling most structured movements but in the process have increased the bitter resentment felt by the student body. The evolution toward chaos can also be partly explained by the fact that when the student movement started, the students had something to oppose: the official university syndicate, SEU. One they had pulled that down it proved difficult, if not impossible, to put something in its place—not only because destroying is easier than building, but mainly because the police and the other authorities did not permit any building to be done.

The Spanish university movement began in 1956. In the preceding period, Ruiz-Jiménez, as Minister of Education from 1951 to 1956, had started a movement of reconciliation in Spanish cultural and university life by opening the cultural institutions, as far as he could, to those who merited positions in them rather than, as had been the case since the Civil War, to those who could prove their political reliability (on the Falangist side). This led to a threefold struggle among the students: the Falangists tried to maintain their political leadership and privileges; the Opus Dei attempted to gain more and more ground; and a democratic student movement, at that time perhaps principally of Catholic inspiration, wanted to refashion the universities. It came to public demonstrations and street fighting, culminating on February 10, 1956, in violent clashes between masses of students demonstrating for and against the Falange and their sindicatos. In the disturbances, a Falangist student was shot; it was never established by whom. Ruiz-Jimenez and Fernandez Cuesta, the minister responsible for the sindicatos, resigned; but the movement for democratically elected student unions was launched.

The students attempted to establish student associations to rival the official SEU. Around 1961 there were two in existence: FLDE (*Federación Libre de Estudiantes*) and UED (*Unión de Estudiantes Democráticos*). The former was Marxist and Castroist in orientation and is said to have been financed in part from abroad. The latter had a Catholic trend. Together, they tried to hold free assemblies of students. Finally, in 1965, the authorities gave in: SEU disappeared from the universities but continued to exist as a coordinating body. A new law authorized the foundation of APE (*Asociaciones Profesionales de Estudiantes*); but, as so often with such concessions in Spanish political life, these were hedged by all kinds of limitations. Students had to swear allegiance to the fundamental laws; each university year had to have its separate association; all associations together were to unite at the top in SEU; and the SEU officers continued to be nominated and not elected.

The students, therefore, continued to agitate for free assemblies and reunions. The monastery of Sarria in Catalonia allowed its premises to be used by one of those assemblies in May 1966. After two days they were expelled by the police, and this led to a protest march of priests in Barcelona, which made history in Spain. Agitation continued to grow, spilling out from the campuses into the streets. Joint actions with the workers were attempted. This went on until the end of 1968. Then, in January

1969, a state of emergency was proclaimed, mainly because of student troubles. It lasted two months, and when it ended police were stationed permanently inside the universities.

This gave the students a new provocation for protests and riots, which continues to the present day. But it also succeeded in reducing the mass movements of the previous period into small, fragmented groups. Policemen were also enrolled as students to spy on their fellow undergraduates, and nobody was safe to speak and act freely except in the company of his closest friends. Policemen with walkie-talkies patrolled the university corridors, called for reinforcements at the slightest disturbance, and broke into any student meeting, beating up the participants. All posters and notices were automatically taken off the walls by the police. Moreover, vigilante groups of pro-Falangist students were encouraged—at least passively, in the sense that nobody checked whether they had arms—to take action against their colleagues.

But order was never truly established. Studies suffer badly as a result of the troubles, but the universities are also bedevilled by a great many purely academic and organizational ills. Above all, they are wildly overcrowded—to such an extent that study becomes a physical impossibility for many students in the larger facilities. Many of the classes are given by assistant professors (*no numerarios*) who do not have the rights of academic staff and are very badly paid. They tend to identify with many of the student complaints and demands. When troubles become too widespread, faculties, and even whole universities, are closed down. In the past few years, the universities of Madrid and Barcelona have been open for less than half of each academic year.

The politically minded students are small minorities. But no student can go through a Spanish university without feeling badly and unjustly treated by the police and by those in authority on many occasions. Thus the universities become schools of disaffection from the regime. With a minority of students, the alienation turns into active opposition politics. There is a great number of constantly changing political groups. For a considerable time, FLP (*Frente de Liberación Popular*) was fashionable. The *Felipes,* as they were called in university slang, considered that Spain was ripe for revolution, but that the traditional parties, including the PCE, did not know how to go about it. Their aim was Socialist revolution. But they have now quieted down. Today there are Maoists, Trotskyites, Communists, Socialists, Social Christians, Democratic Christians, Castroists, and Falangists of the whole spectrum. Although the predominant tone of the political students is clearly Marxist, the varieties of Marxism are many, and the forcing of political groups with the universities to shrink to the size of cells has increased divergent tendencies.

The regime has attempted several reforms of the universities and of the whole educational system. But thus far these seem to have intensified the difficulties. There was large-scale educational reform under Minister of Education Villar Palasi (1968 – 1973) and his deputy, Diez Hochleitner, previously the UNESCO specialist on educational planning. This started with great promise. A White Paper was published in 1969 which attempted to diagnose all the ills of Spanish education and promised changes and remedies for all of them. This was followed by the enactment of an Educational Law by the Cortes. The education minister tried to get the budget required for the reforms incorporated into the law and thus assured for the future. But he failed; the Budget and Finance Committee of the Cortes retained its control over this matter. After this initial divergence between promise and reality, the reform ran into increasing difficulties. Those who were anxious to put it into operation tried to improvise solutions where the material resources were lacking or when not enough qualified specialists could be found. The result was a considerable amount of chaos. This provoked protests from pupils and students, as they became more and more uncertain about the kind of academic work expected from them and the conditions under which they had to study. The regulations kept changing and the material conditions grew steadily worse as ever-increasing numbers of students, insufficiently prepared, tried to crowd into the state schools and universities. The attempt to secure more rigorous discipline in the universities by the Council of Ministers— a decree issued during the summer of 1972 making professors responsible for discipline and at the same time subordinated them directly to the Council itself—made no discernible difference. Riots and protests continued just as before.

The latest Minister of Education, Martínez Esteruelas, apparently realized the need to reduce the excessive pressure of new entrants into universities unable to cope with the ever-growing numbers of students, and decided that there must be greater selectivity. This was undoubtedly a reasonable and courageous decision, but it immediately gave the students new cause for protest. In fact, one year of high-school graduates had been enrolled into the newly created pre-university year, the *cursos universitarios de orientación,* known as CUO, without being told that at the end of that year they would have to pass a competitive examination in order to enter the universities proper. Moreover, anything resembling a *numerus clausus* arouses suspicions of class favoritism among the students and evokes protests against the undemocratic attitude of the authorities.

At the time of writing, a University Law was in the process of being drafted, but it is unlikely that the problems of the Spanish universities will be resolved in the near future. Their root lies in the fact that Spanish youth is deeply alienated from the regime, and academic youth most of all. The trouble is compounded by the well-nigh impossible conditions of study at the universities; perhaps only in Southern Italy are they as grievous. Finally, all the academic professions experience serious problems with the regime, so that students see ahead of them, after university, a further indefinite period of difficulty and struggle with the authorities. The kind of professional troubles that reflect on the universities are those of: the doctors, who have to work in under-equipped, badly organized state hospitals and clinics; the architects, as a result of the rampant speculation in urban real estate; the lawyers, whose professional associations are dominated by old-time Falangists, not to speak of the public order tribunals, and other special judicial bodies; and the teaching profession, underpaid, and plagued by the chaotic state of the school and university system. The list of the complaints of the younger generation of professionals is a very long one and fills a good deal of the daily newspaper space. The one basic is an older generation that occupies the leading positions and is maintained in them with the help of the state. The younger people regard the situation as inefficient, outdated, corrupt, and hypocritical.

The Basques and ETA

The Basques and the Catalans really merit separate and much more elaborate treatment; in the present context, however, only the most outstanding current movements in the two nations can be mentioned.

The special position of the Basques in Spain remained relatively well preserved under the *fueros,* or local rights, till the period of the Carlist wars. The three Carlist wars allowed the "liberals" in the capital to limit the extent of this traditional and somewhat medieval position of legal privilege in favor of Madrid centralism. In the late romantic period, toward the end of the 19th century, Basque nationalism emerged, based principally on the Basque language. Its founder was Sabino Arana Goiri, who was born in Bilbao in 1865. Arana's nationalism was deeply Catholic and conservative. In 1894 he founded the *Partido Nacionalista Vasco* (PNV), which until recently remained the chief proponent of Basque nationalism. The Basque clergy were often enthusiastic collaborators of the PNV, while its important political antagonists were the Socialists in the industrial city of Bilbao and the Carlists, mainly in the province of Navarre.

During the Republic and the first years of the Civil War, the PNV forged an alliance with the Socialist Prieto and became one of the constituent groups of the government in Madrid. In the autonomous state of *Euzkadi,* Aguirre of the PNV became president. He died in exile in 1960. After the war, which ended for them in 1937, the Basques lost all their privileges. Navarre was able to keep its fueros and retain its own local autonomy, because the province—with the Carlist *Requetés*—had fought on the Nationalist side.

ETA (*Euzkadi ta Askatasuna,* Euzkadi and Freedom) grew out of the PNV. Its younger generations at first formed groups within the veteran nationalist party. Later, they detached themselves from it and 1959 finally saw the move of most of the young people from the PNV to the new organizations. In all the earlier writings of the ETA one finds the Algerian rising taken as the model. The founding years of the ETA occurred while the struggle of the Algerian provisional government (GPRA) was finally nearing success after years of fighting against a superior military power which, according to the predictions of the specialists, it could never hope to overcome. The mixture of radical nationalism and radical socialism which had become apparent in Algeria's case was just what the young Basque nationalists aspired to. Their movement was born of impatience with the passive attitude of their elders in the PNV; they wanted to be much more active, and the activists stamp has remained on the movement. The members require constant activity in order to prove to themselves and their opponents alike that the movement is still alive. Whether this activity contributes to the strategy of liberation for Spain or of the Basque country is quite often of only secondary importance, or is simply not given much thought.

Even though armed struggle was their intention from the start, the young men of ETA did not shed blood for many years. They began by painting slogans on the walls, like the famous $3 + 4 = 1$, meaning that the three French Basque provinces and the four Spanish ones were to be one country. Later, they began setting off harmless bombs in front of Guardia Civil barracks and blowing up monuments of Falangist Civil War heroes. Their first congress took place in 1962 and formulated a socialist and nationalist program. The fifth congress in 1967 was of great importance, because it produced a split between the more nationalist and the more socialist factions. The nationalists claimed that the fight against Spain and for the freedom of the Basque country was to have precedence. The "scientific socialists" maintained that only in the context of a Spain freed from capitalism would there be any chance of building a Basque socialist homeland, and consequently declared themselves solidly with the Spanish working class. The sixth congress, in 1970, ratified the split. The "scientific socialists" were in the majority and expelled the Basque nationalists when the latter accused them of "Marxism and Hispanism". The nationalists, among whom were numbered some of the founders of ETA, claimed "the legality of the Fifth Congress" and took the name *ETA V* or *ETA militar*. At the fifth congress, the organization had been divided into four branches: Workers' Front, which was to gain influence among the Basque workers; Cultural Front, which was to occupy itself with Basque culture and language; Political Front, whose purpose was to unite the different political groups in the Basque country; and Military Front, which was to undertake the bombing and shooting attacks. The Marxist sixth congress decided for political work and against terrorism. Once again the members split up into different factions. As far as is known, they are busy with political work, chiefly in the factories.

One of the problems of all Basque nationalists is the very considerable influx of Spaniards, mostly from Andalusia, who come to work in the rapidly expanding Basque industries. Naturally, they bring their families along, and a large proportion of them settle permanently in Vizcaya. Should they be treated as foreigners or should the political organizations try to gain supporters from among them? The question is complicated by the language problem. Obviously the new immigrants do not know Basque, and since the language of the schools is Spanish, there is little incentive for them to learn Basque. The more socialist groups stand for the solidarity of all workers, Spanish and Basque, against all capitalists and the capitalist state. The Basque nationalists, however, even though they too are socialists, want to build a solely Basque socialist state. They regard the influx of foreign workers as one of the evil deeds of Madrid, which, in their eyes, is trying to "swamp us with Spaniards".

In the summer of 1968, violence broke out. It began in June with shootings between the Guardia Civil and Basque activists. As an act of revenge, ETA decided to kill a police inspector, chief of the brigada social of San Sebastián, Melitón Manzanas. The Basques maintained that he had approved the torture of political prisoners and had participated himself. The attack on him was carried out successfully in Irún on August 5. On the same day, the government declared a three-month state of emergency for the province of Guipúzcoa (captial San Sebastián). Habeas corpus was suspended, houses could be searched without warrant, and freedom of movement was curtailed. About 50 people were arrested in Guipuzcoa and, according to the Basques, were tortured. According to many sources, political prisoners were beaten frequently and could be thankful if that were the worst that befell them. Many of those prisoners were merely suspects. From the outside it looked as if the police were arresting anyone known to have Basque nationalist sympathies, regardless of whether the individual belonged to the old PNV or to newer activist groups, perhaps in order to make everyone tell what he knew and thus gradually zero in upon the real terrorists. This apparently undiscriminating procedure was bound to increase popular sympathy for ETA and to make the police forces more detested than ever. Priests were among the victims of the police persecution, because many of the Basque priests were sympathetic to Basque nationalism, while others belonged to the progressive Catholic groups. In the end, none of them turned out to have been connected with the murder of Manzanas.

From then on, a running war was maintained between ETA and the police. On January 25, 1969, a state of emergency was imposed on the whole of Spain. In the next two months many ETA people were arrested in the northwestern provinces, Guipúzcoa, Vizcaya, Alava, and Navarre. In the summer of that year began a series of trials conducted by military tribunals in Burgos, with prison sentences of up to 10 and 20 years and life. But the most famous case, causing widespread international concern, did not take place until December 1970. This was the trial of the group of Basques accused of responsibility for the murder of the police chief, Manzanas. The principal accused, Izco, had been captured on January 5, 1969, as he was trying to liberate his fiancée from the provincial prison in Pamplona. The evidence produced by the police to link him with the murder appeared to most independent observers of the trial to be very dubious. Nevertheless, seven death sentences were pronounced in Burgos. There was a big international press campaign against the trial, and the Basques abducted the German Consul in San Sebastián, Beihil, as a hostage. Eventually, the death sentences were commuted to life imprisonment and the consul was released. The international furore over the trial had its repercussions inside Spain. Manifestations took the form of huge demonstrations in favor of Franco, the biggest since 1946; in Madrid the numbers were estimated as high as 150,000. The demonstrations, organized by the Falange and Falangist officers, were not only for Franco and against foreign intervention; they were also against the Opus Dei government, which was accused of having been too soft toward the Basques.

The feud between the police and the ETA activists of the Military Front went on and on. Shootings and arrests, bomb outrages and trials continued throughout 1971 and 1972. In January 1973, there was a spectacular abduction of a Madrid millionaire, Felipe Huarte, who owned factories in Navarre that had been on strike for some time. He was eventually released in France on payment of a ransom and a promise to reinstate the striking workers and accept their demands.

According to police sources, the military branch of ETA held their sixth congress (they did not recognize the one in 1970, which had been dominated by the left wingers) on August 15, 1972, in French Gascony. Among their decisions are said to have been the retention of the military (i.e., terrorist) aspect of the ETA, which was to be intensified by training refugees from the Spanish Basque provinces inside French Basque territory. They allegedly changed their command structure by nominating an executive committee of four, because after the death of Eustaquio Mendizabál, a former leader shot by the police, there had been a feeling of insecurity about the leadership. The four are reported to be: Uturbe Abazolo, Pagoago Gallastegui, Múgica Arregui, and Urruticoechea Bengoechea. Eight commando units, each consisting of four or five men, were to be formed. Political, cultural and propaganda units were also formed, and it was decided to collaborate closely with *Embata*, the organization for Basque refugees on the French side of the border. There is little doubt that the existence of the border is of great value to ETA. The French side gives them a refuge from police persecution, even though French-Spanish official collaboration has been growing over the years.

The greatest coup of ETA was the assassination of the prime minister, Carrero Blanco, in the center of Madrid on December 20, 1973. It was done, according to the organization's spokesman, in order to avenge nine ETA men who had been shot by the police not long before. In addition, they believed that the murder would hasten the decay of the regime "by leading to increased rivalry between the Opus Dei and the Falange". They also claimed that it would be a blow to the succession Franco had arranged for himself. The second reason is more credible than the first. The Opus was definitely removed from Spanish political life with the death of Carrero, its protector, but its participation in the government had already been reduced in June, when the Carrero government was formed. As to the succession, it might have been easier with a man like Carrero, experienced and enjoying Franco's complete trust, than under the new prime minister, Arias Navarro, or his possible successor. But whatever the "ifs" of history, the assassination did not in reality effect a great difference in the Spanish state. Things continued on much on the same course as before. The murder does not appear to have brought ETA appreciably closer to its declared goal, Basque autonomy; on the contrary, it reinforced Madrid's repression of the Basques. It may have helped in giving a boost to the prestige of ETA in extremist circles which admired the technically perfect execution of the plot, but its political relevance seems rather doubtful.

ETA subscribes to the theory that violence will provoke repression, repression, more violence, and that the vicious circle will become wider and wider. The Spanish police, by their methods, seem so far to have collaborated obligingly in making this theory work. But there is little evidence as yet that a sizeable mass of Basques have become alienated from Spain and regard the Spanish "colonialists" as the Algerians regarded the French settlers. The cultural differences are by no means as sharp. The Basque bourgeoisie is quite strong and has its share of the cake of power in the Spanish establishment. There is a long and real tradition of coexistence behind both peoples. There is no wider cultural identity, comparable to Islam or Arabism, to which the Basques could lay claim to reinforce their sense of belonging to a different group than their "colonizers".

There is little doubt that many Basques would welcome financial and legal autonomy or partial autonomy. They are convinced they could manage things better themselves, and are probably right. They can point to the fact that the Basque provinces lead all Spanish provinces (with the exception of the two big cities of Madrid and Barcelona) in per capita income. Many Basques do not see why the taxes they pay should go to subsidize Madrid or the poor parts of the Peninsula. The same is true of cultural autonomy: they would like to be able to print newspapers in Basque, to have Basque primary schools, etc. Nevertheless, there is little evidence that those willing to kill and to be killed for such aims are more than a small minority of young students and intellectuals who have become possessed by their theories.

Many Basques are proud of the deeds of ETA, even though they themselves would not commit them. In a sense, ETA has become a symbol of Basque daring and efficiency. There are many opposition groups that would have liked to assassinate the prime minister, but it was the Basques who brought off the feat. But it is a long step from pride to participation; and so far, one cannot say that the Basque people as a whole have taken it or appear ready to take that step.

If ETA remains a small group, provoking the Spanish police by their needle-pricks, it seems likely that it will contribute to the maintenance of the present regime and its more repressive traits rather than advance the liberation of Spain or of Euzkadi. This is so because any blow to the police forces on the scale of the last few years will serve to harden their attitude and provide ammunition for the hardliners in the regime rather than bring them to their knees. ETA can always hope for a decisive escalation of its "war", but on the evidence of its deeds since 1968, this seems a fairly empty hope. ETA activities would have to be stepped up to such an extent as to turn the current sporadic revolver battles and occasional bomb outrages into a real popular war. There is no evidence that an escalation like this is underway or that, in the present circumstances, it would be at all possible.

Catalonia

Catalonia is more secure in the knowledge of its identity than the Basque country. It is bigger, with nine million Catalan-speaking people in Spain and the French Roussilon. It boasts its own center, Barcelona, an established economic importance, and a settled bourgeois society. Above all, the Catalans went through a renaissance (renaixença) of their language and culture in the 19th century and the beginning of the 20th, which is something the Basque region hoped for but achieved, at best, only sketchily. Perhaps this is why Basque nationalism, feeling insecure and menaced by Spain and the Spanish language, has developed certain frenetic qualities. Catalan nationalism in any case appears not only more settled, more sure of itself, but also more diverse. It does not have one main current, but many. It is just as complex and contradictory a society as Spain, with its distinctive regions—the Roussilon, Catalonia proper, the Balearics, and Valencia—each with its own center.

All Catalans, it is true, bear common grudges against Castille, Madrid, centralism, and Spain. The most general one is linguistic and cultural. Catalan, which was the teaching language before the Civil War, is no longer used in the schools; there is still no Catalan daily or weekly newspaper. Catalan writers and intellectuals deem their language to be threatened with extinction unless it is restored to the educational system. Madrid has allowed books to be published in Catalan, and publishing in Catalan has grown to be an important industry; but the Catalan book is usually more expensive than the Castilian because the editions are smaller. Catalan folk singers have been able to appear, and there are many Catalan records for sale; but radio and television, both state monopolies, devote only a few minutes to Catalan programs each day, simply so as to be able to claim they are not ignoring the language. The Church has used Catalan adequately since the Vatican Council, however, and masses are said in Catalan throughout the country.

The other significant grudge is heard mostly in Barcelona; it concerns taxes. The people of Barcelona and the surrounding industrial cities do not understand that they pay taxes corresponding to the high economic output of their part of the country, and they complain that Madrid spends all their revenues outside Catalonia.

The big city of Barcelona has its Falangist and wealthy industrialists and business people who are sympathizers of the regime and work hand-in-hand with the authorities. Not everybody agreed with the Republicans during the Civil War, and there were always some hidden Franco supporters even during the war years.

Later, they naturally multiplied. But Barcelona also has its well-to-do bourgeois circles which feel profoundly Catalan and for this reason never really accepted the regime. Memories of the postwar period, when people would be stopped in the streets and insulted by some Castilian-speaking Spaniard for talking in their own language, and of times when there were posters ordering them to "Speak the language of the Empire!" are still vivid to this day. From time to time, a Catalan of the opposition under arrest will be beaten because he refuses to answer questions in Castilian and insists on talking Catalan to the police inspector or the public order tribunal. Generally, the political police tend to be even tougher in Catalonia than in the central parts of Spain. This is probably a partially unconscious reaction to the climate of hostility—something of an occupation situation has always persisted in Catalonia.

At the same time, there is a tremendous influx of immigrants into Barcelona and the surrounding industrial cities. Nearly all the immigrants are either from Andalusia, Castilian speaking, or from Galicia, speaking their own Gallego. They are usually humble people, willing to acclimatize themselves to Catalonia; many of them would even like to learn Catalan, or have their children learn it, if they had the opportunity. A sociological bestseller called "The Other Catalans" by Franciso Candel gives an impressive description of their problems (*"Els altres Catalans"*, 1st edition 1964, 6th edition February, 1965, Spanish edition, *Los otros Catalanes, Ediciones Peninsula*, Barcelona, 1965).

The opposition groups in Catalonia are as numerous and as divergent as in any other part of Spain. The Catalan Communist Party, which calls itself PSUC (*Partido Socialista Unificado de Cataluña*), is independent of Santiago Carrillo's PCE, finding it "revisionist". As Barcelona is the old center of Spanish trade-union activity and leftism, the traditional parties which survived the Civil War are stronger here than in the newly industrialized regions. It is said that there has been a revival, clandestine of course, of the old CNT (*Confederación Nacional del Trabajo*) and FAI (*Federación Anarquista Iberíca*). ASO (*Asociación Sindical Obrera de España*) is also considered to be stronger in Catalonia than elsewhere. This is a trade union group mainly of Socialists, but also containing many Catholics who are wary of the Communists. Finally, the remnants of the Socialist UGT (*Unión General de Trabajadores de España*) of Civil War renown are stronger here than in most other regions. But, as in other parts of Spain, the comisiones obreras are of much greater importance than these smaller political groups.

University resistance in Barcelona is even more active than it is in Madrid. In this field, too, Catalan national feeling and resentment against enforced Castilianization adds an extra dimension to the struggle. It is one of the issues which will always rally large groups of students who are not necessarily stirred by left-wing slogans and complaints. The background of Catalan national feeling also helps to knit students and faculty closer together. Much of the modern art life of Barcelona, which is more vital than that of Madrid, also has a resistance flavor. As in other Spanish industrial centers, the main core of opposition in Barcelona, apart from the university, is to be found in the big industrial plants. The Castilians have the monopoly of the export trade to South America.

Barcelona is also the most "European" city of Spain. This is due to its proximity to France and to its many business connections with other parts of the continent. Catalan businessmen have recently begun investing money across the border in France. There is considerable preoccupation with the possibility and necessity of entering the Common Market, and consequently a tendency to measure Spanish institutions against the corresponding European ones; the main problems are always the trade unions and the parties. Links with Italy are also much stronger than Madrid's. While Rome, seen from the Spanish capital, is principally the seat of the Church, Barcelona is aware of Italian industry, Italian intellectual, political, and artistic life. Finally, the annual flow of millions of tourists streaming along the coast and through Barcelona also creates ties with Europe.

All these factors are present in Barcelona without making themselves felt very much in Madrid. The two big cities remain strangely isolated and always seem to be deliberately ignoring one another. Madrid rules and Barcelona resents it, closing itself in and leading its own life on the fringe of Spain.

If ever the central authority in Madrid should become weak, or preoccupied with its own difficulties, it seems likely that there would be a challenge from Barcelona. This would inevitably come from the left, which would try to involve as much of the Catalan lower-middle and middle classes as it could influence. The students would be enthusiastically supportive. But a considerable proportion of the business community would probably be afraid of the red complexion of such a political challenge and see no choice for itself but to uphold the interests of Madrid in order to preserve its wealth and its privileges. The divisions would be very much the same as in the Civil War; but this does not necessarily mean that the left challengers would be able to dominate Catalonia.

Much of the effort's success would depend on the availability of troops and armed police units from the center, which the regime could bring into operation quickly to preserve its power. Any popular Catalan challenge from the left is bound to be disorganized and chaotic at the start, badly armed—if armed at all—and ill-prepared, simply because police supervision in Catalonia is too strict to permit any large-scale preparations. This means that any major uprising would need time to organize its command structure and to arm its recruits. The troops of the Guardia Civil, the armed police, and the army could easily quell it if they were in a position to operate during the first few days. Only a rising left to itself for a considerable period, neglected for some reason by the central powers for weeks rather than days, would have any chance of effecting a permanent change in the existing order. An uprising that failed would mean a more or less radical return to the state of affairs that prevailed immediately after the Civil War, not necessarily in the economic, but certainly in the political field: rigid re-imposition of the Castilian "empire".

A positive way of delivering Catalonia from its present somewhat oppressed condition would be the establishment of a Catalan region, having a certain degree of autonomy, within the framework of a united Europe. But under present circumstances such a proposition belongs to the world of dreams rather than to the realm of practical possibilities.

II. THE EMPTY CENTER

The most outstanding characteristic of the Spanish political system is that it has a small extreme right, working legally, and an energetic extreme left, working illegally, while the center remains politically inactive. The two wings tend to reinforce each other. Falangists (with police support) react against the provocations of the left, and the left attempts to outmaneuver or circumvent the Falangist control of the state syndicates. Both feel that they have a right to represent everybody—the Falangists because they see themselves as Spain, and the left because they believe that they are acting in the interests of the people, or even that, being their vanguard, they are the people themselves.

The center groups, which would probably comprise the largest part of the political spectrum if they could act freely, find themselves reduced to small circles of friends who can meet legally (officially, not more than twelve of them at one time) to discuss political subjects. True, they could organize illegally, just as the Communists or the Maoists do, but in practice they do not organize, or do so inefficiently and inexpertly. This is logical. The workers have a strong motive for organizing, at least rudimentarily, in groups such as the comisiones: their urgent economic need to keep up with inflation or to improve their very low wages. The old and new middle classes have less reason; they are busy professionally, they are on the side of legality and moderation, and consequently, illegal politics are repugnant to them. If they have very strong leanings towards political activity.

there is always a good chance that they will gravitate to one of the two extremes: to the Falangist of Falangistoid government groupings if they are after office, or to the PCE or smaller extreme leftists groups if they are after social justice.

The government has promised to remedy this situation, at least partially, by licensing "political associations in the framework of the National Movement". But so far these promises have not been fulfilled. Even if they were, one would have to wait to see the kind of legal restrictions that would be imposed on the envisaged political associations.

For nearly 35 years now, the empty center has, in a sense, been filled by the person of Franco. He has kept a certain equilibrium between the political forces of the regime, the so-called "political families", changing it according to the demands of the times. He has kept the armed forces outside the political arena, never tolerating their interference, and he has kept the political forces of the left, the losers in the Civil War, in subjection and under the iron control of the police. Because of this crucial role, fulfilled for so long by the Caudillo and Franco's one-man authority, the question that every Spaniard inevitably asks himself is: what will happen to the country when Franco, 81 at the time of writing, is dead or incapacitated?

In theory, there are rules for the succession. Don Juan Carlos has been selected as the future king in a monarchy which is being "instated". This term has been used in order to avoid any hint of "restoration", which might have implied recognition of the former royal family's dynastic right to the throne. The king is to be assisted, and in fact supervised, by the *Consejo del Reino* (Council of the Realm), consisting of 17 high dignitaries of the state and the president of the Cortes. But there is some uncertainty as to whether the two authorities, even acting in concert, can really replace Franco. The danger would be that one or the other of the two political wings, the Falangists or the left, might step in and try to take power into its own hands. As things stand now, there is little chance that the left would be able to seize and keep power, but there is a grave danger that in some way it would make the attempt. If such an attempt were made, and if it were not dealt with speedily and easily by the police, the army would feel bound to intervene, and might then be tempted—or feel obliged—to stay in power under some guise or other. Spain would thus come to be a political system comparable to that which predominated for so long in Greece.

There would be less danger of this happening if the empty center of Spanish politics could be filled by something more than the designated successor and his Council. Perhaps the political associations could do this, but only if they were conceived in a sufficiently broad spirit to permit the free play of the different political tendencies existing in the country. In this admittedly not very probable eventuality there might, for example, be one association of the Monarchists and industrial right, perhaps a second of the more conservative Catholics (DC), and a third of Democractic Socialist leanings. At the end of the liberalizing process, once the system had proved itself, one might even envisage a license for an extreme left-wing association, provided it showed itself willing to abide by the democratic rules. Perhaps, with the passage of the years the name "association" could be changed to "party"—a word prohibited at present by the Spanish fundamental laws. But it is not frames or names that matter; what is important is that there should be a possibility of establishing, whether through the ballot box or some other method, what it is that the majority—or a significant proportion—of the Spanish people want. At present the question of what the Spaniards want is subject to systematic and arbitrary mystification. The Falange claims that "the huge majority" want the present regime to last forever. The left wing groups claim that "the masses" are with them, or certainly would be if they could be properly informed. Whoever seizes power or happens to possess it is in a position to claim that the Spaniards are with him. Nobody can contradict him without risking imprisonment.

The political system could thus be improved ("perfected" is the word the Spaniards prefer) so as gradually to fill the vacuum of the center. It would be safer to do this while Franco is still alive, because he would be able to reinforce the rather delicate process with the weight of his authority. If it were attempted after Franco, there would always be the danger of some of the right-wing forces, or even the army and the police, intervening in order to preserve the Franco system, defined as "the legality of the regime". But—with considerable luck—a gradual change might possibly be brought off, even if it were still proceeding after Franco's disappearance from the scene.

There is, however, the second main pillar of the regime to be considered: the state syndicates. They would be much more difficult to change. The tension inside the sindicatos between the state officials controlling them and the workers and their elected representatives (*enlaces, jurados*) is so great that a liberalization by removing the state controls or even easing them gradually to the point of permitting the workers to decide their own actions and policies, would lead to very violent agitation, to strikes, and quite possibly to a general strike. Spanish workers would want to fight for wages comparable to those of other workers in Europe, at least of the Italians, and this would prompt fairly violent confrontation between workers and employers. Both sides are accustomed by now to the straitjacket restriction of the state syndicates, though it is the workers who have been more stringently contained than the bosses. It is difficult to imagine a general strike, even in one part of Spain alone, without the "forces of order"—police, guardia civil, army—feeling obliged to intervene; and it is equally difficult to envisage them intervening and not reimposing some new controls on the workers. In fact a general strike, particularily if there were some disorders, could easily serve as the pretext for the armed forces taking over power in the name of order and the legality of the regime.

But is it necessary to change the sindicatos system? Could they not remain as they are, and the workers, as economic expansion permits, gradually be paid higher wages? It would probably be difficult to maintain the syndicates if the political system were changed sufficiently to fill the political vacuum of the center. For that change would involve giving the workers a political voice, and they would use it first of all to obtain free trade unions. It seems probably that a very large section of the Spanish middle and lower classes would regard the workers as entirely justified in that demand.

Wise men in the labor force, firmly in command and willing to proceed step by cautious step to a real liberalization, might perhaps be capable of opening up a gradual passage towards trade union freedom without the convulsion of a bitter disorderly and probably violent general strike. They would have to realize that the inevitable intervention of the army would drive the workers back—perhaps not merely to their starting-point, but to an even more intolerable position. But even wise men would need a good deal of luck to be successful, and something like a relatively minor economic recession could cause the collapse of all their careful plans.

Generally speaking, flourishing economic circumstances, such as Spain has begun experiencing in the last few years, would be very helpful in the difficult period of transition (or tense stagnation) that seems bound to follow Franco. A recession or even reduced growth would greatly increase the risks, because of the dangers of social tension. Many more Spaniards are hopeful of economic betterment than of political liberalization. An annual improvement in their economic circumstances is felt by most people to be due them. Because this desire has been gratified to a modest extent over a considerable period, people expect, as their right, to be at least a little bit better off each successive year. This "rising expectations" phenomena is prevalent in many countries in transition, and has often served as a spur to social change.

Another imponderable of considerable importance for the future is the moment of Franco's disappearance or disablement. The military generation of Civil War officers is gradually fading away. The retirement age is 60 up to the rank of colonel, and 62 for more senior ranks. The youngest officers who went right through the Civil War are now 56 and within four to six years of retirement. Many of their seniors have already retired, in particular the so-called African generation which took part in the colonial wars in Morocco. Franco belongs to this generation, having won his reputation as a young officer in these wars, which ended in 1927. In order to participate in them, an officer had to be born not later than 1909. If he became a general, he should have retired in 1971. The Chief of Staff, General Diez-Alegria, born in 1906, is an exception to the rule.

It is said by competent observers that the wars of their youth have decided the outlook of the majority of the Spanish officers (see: Julio Busquets Bragulat, *El Militar de Carrera in España,*

Estudio de Sociología Militar, Ediciones Ariel, Barcelona/Caracas, 1967). Thus every year there are fewer hard-line officers with an outlook conditioned by the Civil War; but the last of the generals who were lieutenants in the war will not retire until 1980. In that year, Franco will be 88. The proportion of officers in the top echelons with a Civil War mentality who will be active in the army at the time of the transition after Franco will obviously be a very significant factor. Looking back today on the years since 1966, the year of the referendum that ratified the Ley Orgánica, the organic law of the state, and looking forward to the innumerable problems that remain to be solved before a peaceful and gradual transition after Franco could be considered reasonably assured, it seems that the last eight years have not been used to the fullest advantage and that political development has not been quick and decisive enough. This conclusion is put forward rather tentatively, because it is possible, after all, that Franco may survive until the end of the present decade; and during that time the promised political evolution could conceivably be effected. But the chance that this will occur is unlikely. It would have been less of a gamble if the evolution had begun immediately after the plebiscite of 1966. By now, Spain could have had political institutions permitting the great majority of the Spaniards to formulate and express their views on the future of their country, and there would be less risk of an adventurous group proclaiming itself the executor of the alleged will of the people. And if a careful transformation of the syndicates had gone hand in hand with the economic growth of the last eight years, the country would have achieved a trade union system in which the workers were free to act according to their wishes and needs.

As things are, however, Spain has gone a considerable way towards becoming a modern industrial society—with a corresponding improvement in the material condition of the professional, middle, and lower-middle classes—but the political system has not kept pace. This imbalance means a considerable danger of disturbances, or even a breakdown of the whole system, at the critical moment when Franco's directing hand is withdrawn.

Why was it that the political and sindicatos system was not permitted to change along with the economic development of

Spanish society? The answers lie in the personal history and feelings of the men who built the regime, and above all of Franco himself. In the impressionable years of young manhood, these leaders acquired a fairly violent dislike of politicians, and especially party politicians. Franco has stated many times that, in his view, most of the evils of Spain during the whole of the 19th and the first part of this century sprang from party politics, party divisions, parties outbidding each other and taking demagogical approaches to all the problems of the country, culminating in the Communist Party working against Spain and for her subordination under a worldwide empire. His own political efforts have always been directed towards trying to blur lines of division "for the good of all Spain", even at the price of prohibiting the various political groups from expressing their views clearly. His political concept could be called imposed consensus. It has worked under him thanks to the horrors of the Civil War, thanks to his authority gained in that war, allowing him to control the controllers of Spain; and finally, thanks to his own political tact, which has allowed him to balance political forces against one another while keeping them from completely expressing their ideas and identities. While such a system had much to recommend it in an agrarian, underdeveloped Spain with a high level of analphabetism, a tradition of flamboyant political leadership by a somewhat egocentric political and military elite, and tremendous social discrepancies, it is hardly likely to suit today's more developed country, with its large new middle class aspiring to the benefits of a consumer society.

Franco has had the tendency to regard Spain as a sick social organism threatened by its own innate failings. Each people, he is fond of saying, has its own demons, and the demons he sees at work in Spain continue to be those he knew in his youth: disunity and blind partisanship.

To some extent, Franco has become a prisoner of the stereotypes corresponding to the description of Spain before and during the Civil War. It was always his nature to go slow and let things work themselves out, with himself merely giving a final push in the direction he wanted. And this tendency has hardened, in his later years, into a reluctance to change a political system that has served him so well and, in his eyes, done so much for the country. He has convinced himself that his is the right system for Spain. He admits that it may need readjusting to keep abreast of the times; but he has become more and more dedicated to the proposition that Franquism must remain, even after he has gone. The fundamentals of Franquism—the prohibition of parties and of "liberal democracy" in general, and the state syndicate system—may have been the best course for Spain before its recent economic transformation. The question remains whether his judgment is as sound when applied to the new and partially industrialized country he himself has helped to create.

If this reading of Franco's notion of his country and the policy required for it is basically correct, it is obvious that any substantial changes in the political system are highly improbable as long as Franco remains in overall control. He has indicated his desire for discussion on improvements and adaptations. But that is probably merely a device to keep the intellectuals and the professional politicians of the regime and those close to it happily occupied. He has also said many times that the essentials of the system are to be considered as immutable, and there is little reason to doubt his sincerity.

It therefore appears that the necessary changes in the political and social structure will only be attempted, if at all, in the inevitably rather unsettled period following his relinquishment of the controls. Conditions may be so insecure that it will be too dangerous for the government to experiment with any changes and caution in this direction may serve to stabilize the regime for a time. But the inner pressures for change are such that any forcible stabilization would carry the threat of a more violent upheaval once the imposed rigidity cracked.

On the whole, the probable outlook for the period after Franco is that, sooner or later, there will be an uprising on political and social grounds, and that the police or the army will intervene to suppress it. This is likely to give the armed forces an even more important role in the system than they enjoy at present. It would take considerable political skill and a good deal of luck to forestall a development of this nature and set Spain on the road to becoming an open society.